OPPOR

in

Physical Therapy Careers

REVISED EDITION

DISCARD

BERNICE R. KRUMHANSL

McGraw·Hill

New York Chicago San Francisco Lisbon London Madrid Mexico City
Milan New Delhi San Juan Seoul Singapore Sydney Toronto

The *McGraw·Hill* Companies

Library of Congress Cataloging-in-Publication Data

Krumhansl, Bernice.
  Opportunities in physical therapy careers / Bernice R. Krumhansl. — Rev. ed.
      p.   cm.
  ISBN 0-07-144853-5
  1. Physical therapy—Vocational guidance.   I. Title.

  RM705.K78   2006
  615.8′2—dc22   2005005478

1 2 3 4 5 6 7 8 9 0   DOC/DOC   0 9 8 7 6 5

ISBN 0-07-144853-5

Interior design by Rattray Design

McGraw-Hill books are available at special quantity discounts to use as premiums and sales promotions, or for use in corporate training programs. For more information, please write to the Director of Special Sales, Professional Publishing, McGraw-Hill, Two Penn Plaza, New York, NY 10121-2298. Or contact your local bookstore.

This book is printed on acid-free paper.

CONTENTS

Foreword

Choosing a career is one of the most important and difficult life tasks. There is so much that is unknown and not yet experienced, but decisions must be made, often in haste and without sufficient information. The more information we have, of course, the easier the decision, whether we choose to follow a certain path or take another one leading in a different direction.

A book such as *Opportunities in Physical Therapy Careers* is a valuable tool for opening up new areas in the mind for consideration, perusal, and meditation. It may lead you to further research and to the discovery that you really have the talent or the interest to pursue the field. Or it may just as firmly convince you that the field is definitely not for you—an equally important decision. In any case, Bernice Krumhansl's book leaves no area unexplored, no fact hidden—it is all here in an engrossing and readable style.

It is not only the reader looking for a vocation who can benefit from this book. It is also a revealing study of what physical therapy is all about for the patient, who is faced with a new problem requiring a form of treatment of which he or she was only vaguely aware. And the student of physical therapy will find new insights and revelations about the field, as Ms. Krumhansl takes us back in time to tell us the fascinating facts about the early forms of physical healing or about the evolution of massage and hydrotherapy from their natural and unsophisticated roots to their high-tech image of today.

I have used an earlier edition of this book successfully in my introductory classes in Physical Therapist Assisting at Cuyahoga Community College. Nowhere is there a more lucid description of the history of the profession, the American Physical Therapy Association, or the dynamics of physical therapy today than can be found in *Opportunities in Physical Therapy Careers*. I recommend it with enthusiasm to all who wish to experience this rewarding health career as it is seen through the eyes of one of the country's most creative practitioners of physical therapy.

Margaret M. Kotnik, M.A., PT
Consultant, Kent State University
Developer, Physical Therapist Assistant Program, On-Site Team Leader
American Physical Therapy Association, Accreditation of Physical Therapist Assistant Programs

Preface

The benefits of working in the field of physical therapy are many and varied. Like most areas of health care today, physical therapy is a field that is very much in demand. It is also one that pays well, offers great personal satisfaction, and is full of challenges and opportunities.

This book offers you everything you need to know to make an educated decision about whether you want to pursue a career in physical therapy. You'll learn what it's like to work as a physical therapist in a private practice and as a physical therapist assistant in a hospital setting. You'll read about educational requirements, what kinds of classes you'll need to take, and how much your schooling is likely to cost. Perhaps more important, you'll discover the qualities most likely to lead to success in the field, so that you can critically analyze your skills and abilities before you commit your time and money toward pursuing your career.

As in any endeavor, education and preparation are the keys to achieving success, both in planning to enter a field and excelling once you've established yourself in it. Picking up this book is the first step in your journey of discovering the world of physical therapy. May your exploration into this exciting and rewarding field be bountiful!

1

History of the Field and Treatment Methods

Physical therapy is arguably one of the oldest methods of medical treatment. Long ago, when a Cro-Magnon man hurt his back lifting a rock, he may have lain on hot sand to relieve the pain. When his arthritic joints ached (and we know he had arthritis from studies of fossilized bones), he may have placed some of the small rocks heating beside his cooking fire on his tender hands and knees because stone retains heat for long periods. When he scraped his arm and it became infected, he probably bathed his wounds in clear, unpolluted running streams. When he stumbled over a fallen tree trunk, he likely rubbed or massaged his sore shin. Cro-Magnon man knew the importance of physical fitness because if he lost his endurance, speed, or sure-footedness, he lost his race—and perhaps his life—to the next predator he met.

Many of the concepts of the field of physical therapy today remain based on these same principles of massage, heat, cold, irrigation, and manipulation of the body. These efforts help put the body in the best position for its natural defenses to work on healing. Again, while some of the concepts are the same, the tools and methods are incredibly different. Physical therapy today is a high-tech field that uses the latest scientific knowledge and technological advances to help people overcome illness and disability. In this chapter, you will learn about the history of physical therapy and the tenets of its practice.

The Use of Heat and Cold

It has long been known that heat has many therapeutic properties; its most plentiful source is the sun. Thousands of years ago, the Egyptians worshipped the sun's healing powers and erected temples to the sun god Ra. The Greeks worshipped Phoebus Apollo as a sun god. In India the Aryans idolized Savitar as a sun god and divine physician, and in Persia, Mithra was the god of sun and healing. In Germany Wotan-Odin was the god of healing, and people called the sun Wotan's Eye; they also had Odin's fields, recovery places with prominent sunlight where the sick went to recuperate. In Peru the Incans used the sun to heat their houses and water as well as to improve their health.

Heat is effective, generally available in some form, and relatively inexpensive and safe to use. The science behind the use of heat to promote relaxation and healing is fairly simple. Heat packs or warm towels are placed on various parts of the body, many times the spine and neck, to promote muscle relaxation and increased blood flow to the tissues. This is particularly good for those with arthritis and stiff muscles, but it can also bring blood rich with white blood cells to the site of an infection.

Sun is not the only form of heat. Over the years, different cultures have used varying means of creating and obtaining sources of heat to apply to various parts of the body. While these methods may seem primitive and strange today, many of the principles are still sound. For example, the Greeks were the first to use fever therapy as treatment, and the Romans were the first to provide pain relief using applications of hot wax. We know that many Roman patients lay on heated sheep hides and rolled from side to side to obtain relief.

One of today's more innovative forms of heat is in the use of ultrasound. On the eve of World War II, German scientists were working on adapting sound waves for use as a therapeutic agent. The war interrupted the program, but in 1949 seventy-five scientists issued reports on the results of research projects on sound. By the mid-1950s, ultrasound was an important treatment modality. Ultrasound is a form of deep tissue heating in which sound waves are used to penetrate the skin and reach internal body tissues. Ultrasound techniques are best suited for acute pain relief and to promote tissue healing.

The European industrial revolution was a period of tremendous growth in new techniques and advances in crafts, commerce, and business. This was a time when techniques for treating illnesses were constantly being invented and refined. Often, everyday objects were put to use for a variety of purposes—some of which may seem shocking to us today. For example, soon after commercial bakeries were established in France, doctors began ordering "stoving" for arthritic patients. In this process, the patient was placed into a hot oven after the baked bread had been removed. Saunas or steam rooms—essentially the same thing—are still popular today in health clubs, spas, and bathhouses.

A popular treatment in more recent years has been cold therapy, or the use of ice or cold to promote healing. Although Roman emperors used snow to cool water and wine and a few Persian caliphs and emirs enjoyed sherbets, the use of ice for various purposes was never widespread because it could not be produced artificially until 1750. Early Russians used ice more extensively because it was plentiful. They used ice packs to reduce high fevers, to control infections, and to treat wounds and meningitis. They also used it to treat diseases of the central nervous system. During the Russian campaign, Napoleon's surgeons observed that amputations performed on frozen legs were easier, less bloody, and generally more successful than other methods. Arthritic Russians and those suffering from gout responded well to ice in the 1800s, but only recently has this treatment for arthritis been put to use in America.

Today, ice packs or ice massages are most often applied to painful areas to reduce swelling and pain. Both heat and ice are used to reduce muscle spasm and inflammation. A typical course of treatment with heat or ice would consist of applying packs to the injured site for ten to twenty minutes every two hours following an injury. As with most forms of medical treatment, the earlier an injured person receives treatment, the more likely it is to be beneficial.

Hydrotherapy

Water was probably first used for healing purposes when primitive people bathed their wounds in running streams, rinsing out dirt, damaged tissue, and foreign debris. Later the religions of some cultures endowed water with sacred healing properties. The Hindus believed that the Ganges River and six other sacred waters had healing power. Egyptians conferred the same status on the Nile. The Greeks made frequent use of baths in treating wounds, and we read in Homer that the wounded Hector was cured in this way. Galen used water to treat his wounded and injured athletes. Many Native American tribes and traditional Chinese healing systems used sweat baths and other rituals involving water therapies, some of which are still in use today.

Hydrotherapy or the use of water in the treatment of disease has long been in use in the form of baths and spas. The Romans were the first people we know of who made extensive use of hydrotherapy. They had eight hundred public baths at one time, charging adults a small fee and admitting children free. They had sweat houses with hot and cold rooms—the forerunners of the modern Turkish bath. The Romans were also the first to use underwater exercises in warm springs to treat paralysis from war wounds, as well as the pains of normal aging in the civilian population. In modern times, the spas of Europe have become famous health resorts, and the hot springs in many parts of the United States are treatment centers. The Scandinavians, especially the Finns, have used sauna baths extensively, and this, too, has become a popular treatment in the United States.

The first documented use of hydrotherapy in military medicine was during the French revolution, when a surgeon reported his success in treating wounds with large quantities of hot water. At approximately the same time, an Austrian peasant, injured by a fall from a horse, treated himself with hot packs similar to those he used on his animals. His cure was so spectacular that he became famous and began teaching foreign physicians his method. Today we use Hydrocollator packs to relieve pain and heal the sick.

The science behind hydrotherapy is similar to that of heat and cold therapy since the two are enmeshed. Nerve impulses on the skin's surface are transmitted to deeper body tissues where they stimulate the immune system, slow down the production of stress hormones, invigorate blood circulation and digestion, and lessen inflammation. In addition, water negates the effects of gravity, reducing the natural stress on weight-bearing muscles and joints. Hydrotherapy is principally used to stimulate digestion and circulation, reduce stress and anxiety, and provide pain relief. Techniques include still baths or baths with jet streams, sitz baths, showers, footbaths, steam inhalation, and hot and cold compresses.

Electrotherapy

The use of electricity for therapy originated in 641 B.C. when Thales of Miletus discovered that amber, when rubbed vigorously, attracted light-in-weight objects to itself. Also in ancient times, a number of people claimed healing properties from contact with electric eels, electric catfish, and other fish known to give off electric shocks. (This electrical property of some fish species is presumed to be a method of self-defense, so any healing properties would be one of nature's strange accidents.) Eventually, a Roman official suggested the deliberate application of electric fish to gain the benefits of the shock.

Until approximately 1600 no real advances were made in the use of electricity in medicine. Then British scientists William Gilbert and Gilbert Colchester began to conduct research on electrotherapy, and Dr. Colchester eventually published a treatise titled "de Magnete." At about the same time, John Wesley wrote the first book in English on electrotherapy. While each generation and each nation since has contributed to the development of electrotherapy, the great heroes in this area are Luigi Galvani, Michael Faraday, and Alessandro Volta.

When electricity became a part of everyday living, life changed dramatically, and so did medicine. Scientists were able to produce heat and cold and to regulate temperatures. In 1934 an unknown scientist developed heat using a high-frequency current called long-wave diathermy. It was subsequently improved to short-wave diathermy for more effective treatment and easier application. This is the same form of heat as the inductotherm used in steel mills. More recently, Dr. Frank Krusen, a physiatrist at the Mayo Clinic, produced another method of using extremely short waves, which he called microwaves.

Since its inception, electrotherapy has been a common treatment for pain relief, and recent scientific studies have verified that it is an effective form of relief from both chronic and acute pain. That said, the exact mechanism behind the beneficial effects achieved from electrotherapy remains elusive. It is thought that electrical stimulation blocks transmission of pain signals along nerves. One thing that is certain is that electrical stimulation helps release endorphins, the body's natural painkillers.

Electrical stimulation is delivered to the body in the form of high- or low-frequency waveforms or currents. Several different devices that produce such currents exist on the market. They include Transcutaneous Electrical Nerve Stimulation, Interferential Current, and Galvanic Stimulation devices. All of these devices operate in essentially the same way, applying electrical stimulation to nerves and muscles via adhesive pads placed on the skin.

Massage and Exercise

Massage and exercise have long been used to promote health, treat ailments, increase flexibility, and strengthen the body. An ancient, and unfortunately anonymous, medical historian wrote, "Nature early taught man to knead his flesh and bend his body to relieve him of certain ills." In 3000 B.C., Kong-Fu, a Chinese practitioner, wrote a book on the value of massage and exercise. The Japanese also used massage extensively during the same period. The Hindus were among the first to use therapeutic exercises. In the Vedic legends, which are the origin of the Hindu religion, there are detailed descriptions of postural exercises to cure specific diseases. Today in India, Ayurvedic physicians still rely on yoga positions to cure physical and mental illnesses.

Ancient Greek gymnasts were teachers of massage and exercise. They directed the treatment of fractures, dislocations, and other traumatic injuries. Greek physicians gained much of their knowledge from gymnasts. Galen (A.D. 130–201), who gave the first accurate description of bones and muscles, was the surgeon of the Roman gladiators. There are frequent references in the Bible and in Greek and Roman poetry to "anointing with oils," undoubtedly a form of massage.

During the Dark and Middle Ages of Europe, medicine was kept alive in the Western world in the Arab-dominated areas. Several Islamic physicians refer to the use of massage and exercise. In the thirteenth century, two Middle Eastern authors reported on the hygienic and therapeutic effects of exercise. In the sixteenth century, there were three major works on the value of physical agents, massage, and exercise in the treatment of diseases and injuries. By the seventeenth century, two of England's famous surgeons were writing about the value of exercise, and by the middle of the eighteenth century, French and German physicians were writing of the effect of massage on circulation and general health.

The story of therapeutic exercises in modern times is tied closely to the life of Sweden's Pehr Henri Ling (1776–1839). Ling studied theology and had a brief career in the navy before he received an appointment as master of fencing at the University of Lund in 1805. Here he studied anatomy, physiology, and the natural sciences and then developed and taught a new system of movement much different from that of the ancient Greeks, which was still popular in Sweden. Ling demonstrated that properly employed exercise could remedy disease and bodily defects. In 1813 he established the Central Institute of Massage and Corrective Exercises in Stockholm, the first of many institutes for medical and orthopedic gymnastics throughout Europe and the United States. Resistive exercises originated with the Swedish system, as did isometric exercises. Isometric exercises are muscle-building exercises involving muscular contractions (squeezing) against resistance without movement. In other words, the muscles contract but the length of the muscle does not change.

In 1889 a Swiss physician, H. S. Frenkel, introduced a series of exercises for patients with certain diseases that affected the nerves and balance centers. He was the first person to use exercises for the purpose of coordination. Many of these exercises for promoting balance and coordination remain an important part of health care today. Patients experiencing vertigo, or dizziness, have a greater risk of falling. Repeated bouts of vertigo may reduce inner ear function, which leads to a deteriorating sense of balance. Certain exercises can help patients maintain inner ear function, improving their quality of life.

In massage, acupuncture, and acupressure, specific points in the body are kneaded, pressed, and poked with pins to promote health and healing. The Chinese have used acupuncture for many centuries to treat a variety of diseases and as an anesthetic. During a painless procedure, a needle is inserted into specific points in the fourteen meridians, or vertical lines, in the body. The Japanese applied pressure to the same points and called their method Shiatsu, or acupressure. Today physical therapists use acupressure and electrical stimulation on the same ancient Chinese acupoints.

The theory behind massage, acupuncture, and acupressure is that the human body is a complex but interconnected organism. Nerves and blood vessels connect all organs within the body system. The central nervous system and the circulatory system connect internal organs to the skin and all points in between. Pressure applied to certain points in the body will result in electrical messages or bodily fluids carried to other parts.

Physical Therapy as a Profession

As therapeutic medicine developed into a more sophisticated profession, practitioners formed various specialties to concentrate on conquering specific diseases. One such group, called *orthopedists*, treated patients who had problems with bones, joints, and muscles. Orthopedists knew the value of heat to relieve pain, massage to relax muscle spasm, and exercises to strengthen and stretch weak muscles and joints. Unfortunately, applying the combination of heat, massage, and exercise to specific patient problems proved too time-consuming for many orthopedists with busy practices. As a result, toward the end of the nineteenth century, British orthopedists selected young women who were graduates of schools of physical education to administer these special treatments. Because of their physical education background, they had a knowledge of anatomy, physiology, and kinesiology (muscle function). The orthopedists trained them on the job, as apprentices, to direct the special corrective exercises of orthopedic patients.

In the United States, the founding practitioners of physical therapy were also women, although the circumstances surrounding their introduction to practice were slightly different from their English counterparts. From 1915 to 1917, a polio epidemic swept the United States. During this time, Dr. Robert Lovett of Vermont copied the British example and trained two women, Wilhelmine Wright and Janet Merrill, in the muscular reeducation techniques for the treatment of poliomyelitis or, as it was then called, infantile paralysis. In 1917 the United States entered World War I. Battle casualties most frequently involved orthopedic injuries of arms and legs. Because physical training and muscle reeducation were not a part of nursing, medical, or surgical care, the surgeon general's office formed a new department. It was called the Women's Auxiliary Aides, under the division of orthopedic surgery, and it assumed responsibility for this phase of caring for the wounded.

When World War I began, there were no established schools of physical therapy in the United States. The only qualified person in the army was Marguerite Sanderson, who quickly organized a crash course in physical therapy at Walter Reed Hospital. As soon as the battle casualties began arriving, it was obvious that the army would need more therapists than one school could produce. Soon fourteen more schools opened in different parts of the country. Their graduates received a new title: reconstruction aide.

Mary McMillan was an outstanding leader in the development of physical therapy education in this country, and she was generally instrumental in fostering the progress of physical therapy as a profession. During World War I she directed the training of reconstruction aides at Reed College in Eugene, Oregon. This college produced the largest number of graduates during the war.

During the two war years, fourteen schools trained eight hundred physical education teachers to become reconstruction aides, and three hundred of them served overseas. At the beginning of the war they served with the army as civilians. Although they had to obey all the military rules, they did not receive any of the military benefits. Byron's line "Among them, not of them" seems to describe their plight. When the war ended, civilian practice wasn't ready for the specialty of physical therapy. The reconstruction aides returned to the teaching of physical education or to other occupations.

A few schools continued teaching physical therapy. Dr. Frank Granger, who was a staunch advocate of physical therapy, and Mary McMillan codirected a course of study at Harvard Medical School. This course emphasized electrophysics, electrotherapy, and muscle reeducation.

When the country had adjusted to civilian life, a few of the reconstruction aides met for dinner at Keene's Chop House in New York City on January 15, 1921, to form an organization that they called the American Women's Physical Therapeutic Association. Its 245 members elected Mary McMillan as their president. In March 1921 they began publishing a quarterly journal to inform members of the newest advances in physical therapy. By 1928 the Physical Therapy Review was being published bimonthly, and in 1931, after the first decade of its existence, the organization had 534 members. By the end of the 1930s, when they decided to include men in the group, they changed the name to the American Physiotherapy Association. The group now included nearly 1,000 members.

The American Medical Association in 1925 established a Council on Physical Therapy. It outlined courses to be given in medical schools. Graduate nurses and graduates from schools of physical education were accepted for a nine-month course. By 1940 there were sixteen schools graduating 135 students a year. One school had begun to offer a bachelor's degree course. The field of physical therapy was gaining momentum. There were approximately one thousand active therapists and two hundred inactive therapists in the United States.

The entrance of the United States into World War II created an urgent need for a greater number of therapists than the existing schools could possibly supply. To meet this need, seven army hospitals and several private hospitals instituted courses, and fifteen civilian schools accelerated their courses. When the war ended, most of the schools discontinued the short emergency courses, but by 1946 twenty-one schools had a capacity for 480 students.

To avert some of the problems of World War I, Congress declared in December 1942 that a qualified physical therapist would receive the rank of second lieutenant in the army. Women holding a bachelor's degree who had graduated from approved schools of physical therapy were eligible for a commission in the Women Appointed for Voluntary Emergency Service (WAVES). During the war, sixteen hundred women served in the army and eight hundred went overseas.

The war record of physical therapists is inspiring. The Japanese captured and imprisoned several physical therapists, one of whom was Mary McMillan. When the Japanese bombed Pearl Harbor, she was in Manila waiting for a ship to take her back to her teaching post at the Medical College in Peking. She went to the army hospital immediately and volunteered to serve for the duration of the war as a physical therapist. Yet her second army stretch lasted only a few days because she spent nearly all the war years in the Santo Tomas prison camp, where she tried to aid and comfort other prisoners.

In 1944 the United States suffered another bout of polio, this time the worst polio epidemic in history, lasting into the 1950s and totaling approximately 14,500 cases. In 1945 the National Foundation for Infantile Paralysis gave the American Physiotherapy Association $1,267,000 for two thousand scholarships to train physical therapists and other necessary personnel. Simultaneously, the therapists at Warm Springs, Georgia, were developing many new treatment procedures for polio. Many of these treatments were discovered to be applicable to a variety of disease and mechanical problems in addition to polio. By the end of the 1940s, the association once again changed its name to the American Physical Therapy Association.

The 1940s were important years for physical therapy. Battlefront casualties, industrial accidents in defense plants, and polio epidemics brought the attention of the public to the necessity for physical therapy. Physical therapy was no longer a pioneer field. In the 1950s several baccalaureate programs were developing, and graduate school courses were being planned.

As the number of physical therapists increased, the strength of the American Physical Therapy Association grew. Today there are seventy-five thousand members of the APTA throughout the United States. Founded in 1921, *Physical Therapy*, the journal of the American Physical Therapy Association, has received an award for excellence in its category. In 1971 the APTA celebrated its fiftieth anniversary in Boston, looking back to its years of challenge and rejoicing in its achievements. The succeeding years brought even more exciting periods of development and change.

Today we stand on the brink of new research. Biomechanical engineers are devising new types of braces and artificial limbs. Physiatrists are developing many new kinds of equipment that represent dramatic improvements to relieve pain. Several research centers are working on programs using computerized equipment to enable paralyzed patients to become partially independent. New information on muscle function and neurology has increased the efficacy of rehabilitation programs in many areas.

Caring for the Disabled

Everyone, no matter what his or her physical abilities and challenges, is a person with the same basic emotions, desires, and drives. Among these is independence and self-reliance. For many of the physical therapist's patients, although total independence is the patient's goal, the damage caused by a disease or injury may be irreparable. In such a case, the rehabilitation plan must teach the patient to live with the disability.

The word *disability* is not synonymous with words such as *disease*, *injury*, or *defeat*. Physical therapists often use the word *disability* to describe the conditions of patients that, in some way, make them unable to achieve optimal levels of physical functioning. Such conditions often prevent patients from living independently and can make them physically, emotionally, and financially dependent on others. While diseases, injuries, or physical defects may cause disabilities, the presence of such conditions is not always considered a disability. In addition, disability can result when a condition is inadequately treated or when a condition is mismanaged. The rehabilitation of the disabled is now emerging as a major challenge to modern society, and the associated health professions must unite to meet this challenge.

The combination of religious, ethical, and social development in the United States today has resulted in our recognition of the responsibility of caring for disabled citizens by providing them with housing, food, and medical care if they cannot provide these things for themselves. Few private citizens have the financial resources to assume care of another person burdened with large medical bills. The federal government and every state government provide for medical aid and vocational training for the disabled. At the national level, the Department of Health has investigated problems, and laws like the Americans with Disabilities Act protect the rights of the disabled of all ages both in urban and rural communities.

Funding for federal and state programs varies from year to year because it is tied to the federal and state budgets. Therefore, the availability of these services also changes from year to year and from one geographic region to another. As our nation ages and the number of persons who could benefit from physical therapy grows, the federal and state programs will face difficult choices about how to ensure quality care and how to fund it.

Given the cost of physical therapy and the growing demand for services, we must be realistic about patient outcomes. Physical therapists can help by getting to know patients and their families and by helping them set goals. While a full recovery is always the number one goal, it will never be possible or practical for every patient. Therefore, some patients may decide to work in a sheltered shop where they perform simple repetitive motions in a noncompetitive environment and earn a minimal salary. Some patients learn to manage a house, so that their spouses can maintain paid employment outside the home. Some patients never advance beyond basic activities of eating and personal hygiene, and some remain dependent on complete custodial care in a nursing home.

Rehabilitation is not a magic word. It began with a philosophy, became an objective, and developed into a method of coordinating the services of several specialties in the allied health fields. Those who work in rehabilitation have serious responsibilities because they must blend academic scientific knowledge with wisdom born of experience and boldness born of faith. Physical therapy is not a panacea for all that ails human beings, but it is a rewarding and satisfying field that brings great good to many in need and one that you will not regret entering.

2

Is Physical Therapy the Field for You?

HEALTH CARE TODAY is a broad field filled with a spectrum of professionals, many of whom specialize in a particular area of care. Gone are the days when the family practitioner would treat everything from warts and acne to broken bones and intestinal problems. Today's general practitioner serves as a kind of gatekeeper to the vast world of health care. He or she will often be the first person you see for a problem, but then will refer you to a specialist who can develop and implement a plan of care specific to your needs. Physical therapists are one of these specialists.

Physical Therapy Defined

The term *physical therapy* literally means "treatment with physical agents." Historically this therapy was described as "the diagnosis and treatment of disabilities and diseases by the use of physical agents." But what does this mean?

The physical therapist's job, while complex as any occupation dealing with the human body is likely to be, is fairly easy to understand. Physical therapists provide services that help restore body function, improve mobility, relieve pain, and prevent or limit permanent disabilities of patients suffering from injuries or disease. They restore, maintain, and promote overall fitness and health. Their patients include accident victims and individuals with disabling conditions such as low back pain, arthritis, heart disease, fractures, head injuries, and cerebral palsy. Some physical therapists treat a wide range of ailments; others specialize in areas such as pediatrics, geriatrics, orthopedics, sports medicine, neurology, and cardiopulmonary physical therapy.

What the Job Entails

Physical therapists examine patients' medical histories and then test and measure patients' strength, range of motion, balance and coordination, posture, muscle performance, respiration, and motor function. They also determine patients' ability to be independent and reintegrate into the community or workplace after injury or illness. Next, physical therapists develop treatment plans describing a treatment strategy, its purpose, and its anticipated outcome.

Treatment often includes exercise for patients who have been immobilized and lack flexibility, strength, or endurance. Physical therapists encourage patients to use their own muscles to increase their flexibility and range of motion before finally advancing to other exercises that improve strength, balance, coordination, and endurance. The goal is to improve how an individual functions at work and at home.

Physical therapists also use a variety of instruments, including electrical stimulation, hot packs or cold compresses, and ultrasound to relieve pain and reduce swelling. Traction or deep-tissue massage is another method used to relieve pain. Physical therapists also teach patients to use assistive and adaptive devices, such as crutches, prostheses, and wheelchairs. They also may show patients and their families exercises to do at home to expedite recovery.

As treatment continues, physical therapists meticulously document the patient's progress, conduct periodic examinations, and modify treatments as necessary. Besides tracking the patient's progress, such documentation identifies areas requiring more or less attention. It is also a legal document and may be used in a court of law to prove whether a physical therapist has provided care that caused a patient additional injury.

Physical therapy has often been called the cornerstone of rehabilitation because the long road back from injury or disease begins with physical therapy treatments to relieve pain and restore function. If the therapist is to give each patient complete and comprehensive care during the long process of rehabilitation, he or she cannot work in a vacuum. A physical therapist must work closely with the physician, occupational therapist, social service worker, speech pathologist, psychologist, orthopedist and prosthetist, and vocational guidance worker, in addition to a bevy of administrative, medical, and nursing assistants.

The Role of the Physical Therapist Assistant

A physical therapist assistant works with the same kinds of patients that a physical therapist does, but the job duties and responsibilities are quite different. A physical therapist can perform all the treatments that an assistant can perform, but an assistant cannot perform all the treatments that a physical therapist can give. The role of the assistant is neither subservient nor demeaning. The assistant offers an extension to the arms of the therapist to ensure that all patients' needs are met. The assistant may not evaluate or assess a patient, nor make judgments pertaining to therapy, except in simple, routine situations. In some states, the assistant may not work unless a therapist is on duty to give direct supervision. In others, it is possible for the assistant to treat a patient after the therapist has performed the initial evaluation, even though the therapist may not be present.

Job duties and definitions change over time. Some authorities are forecasting that physical therapists will soon be acting as department directors—supervising, evaluating, teaching, and administering—while the assistant performs the more routine duties related to direct patient care. Other leaders point out that many hospitals with limited budgets prefer to employ therapists whose broader educational bases qualify them for a wider scope of activity, authority, and responsibility. In 1985, Medicare and Blue Cross began an intensive cost-cutting campaign in hospitals. The lower salary of the physical therapist assistant may increase the job potential for this group of employees. Duties of the assistant include providing whirlpool and Hubbard tank therapy; diathermy; infrared, paraffin, and ultraviolet therapy; intermittent pressure; ultrasound treatments; massage; cervical and lumbar traction; training in exercises and ambulation; teaching activities of daily living; and assisting the physical therapist in some of the more complicated treatments. If you become an assistant, you will have the opportunity to instruct patients in situations where the information is standardized. You will treat patients under circumstances in which rapid or unexpected adjustments are unlikely and where certain vital signs are readily identifiable and easily interpreted. This level of the profession requires some decision-making and use of judgment, but it does not deal with crucial or demanding situations.

The rest of this chapter offers things to consider and qualities you must possess to excel in this field. While the language used may seem to be particular to physical therapists, much of the same holds true for those who intend to become physical therapist assistants.

Things to Consider

Because you are reading this book, you have likely already thought about becoming a physical therapist and are now seeking more information about the career. But have you ever seriously considered why you are thinking of becoming a physical therapist? Is it because you, or someone dear to you, recovered more rapidly from an accident or illness after physical therapy relieved pain and restored function? Are you a high school or college athlete who wishes to use your motor skills and knowledge of coordination and endurance to help another person walk and become independent again? Do you desire a health career that will challenge your intellect and allow you to provide hands-on patient care without requiring the long years of study necessary to become a physician?

Choosing a career is one of the most important decisions you will ever have to make. It will influence not only how much money you earn for your living, but also where you live and practice and the people you will spend the majority of your week with. Because choosing a career has such long-reaching and all-encompassing effects, the decision must be both emotional and practical. It is a topic you should think long and hard about to avoid wasting time and money on a profession that provides you with no satisfaction or joy.

Practically speaking, you must consider the job outlook, number of hours you will be likely to work each week, and earning potential and evaluate how these factors fit with the lifestyle you envision for yourself. Spending many years and many thousands of dollars preparing for a career in an already overpopulated profession is neither sound nor sensible. Fortunately, the job outlook for physical therapy is excellent.

Employment of physical therapists is expected to grow faster than the average for all occupations through 2012. While the impact of proposed federal legislation imposing limits on insurance reimbursement for therapy services may adversely affect the short-term job outlook for physical therapists, over the long run, the need for physical therapists should continue to rise as the growing number of individuals with disabilities spurs demand for their services. The baby-boom generation is entering the prime age for heart attacks and strokes, increasing the demand for cardiac and physical rehabilitation. Young people will need physical therapy as technological advances save the lives of a larger proportion of newborns with severe birth defects. Finally, future medical developments will permit a higher percentage of trauma victims to survive, creating additional demand for rehabilitative care.

Today, physical therapists hold about 137,000 jobs. The number of jobs is greater than the number of practicing physical therapists, because some physical therapists hold two or more jobs. For example, some may work in a private practice but also work part-time in another health care facility. Most full-time physical therapists work a forty-hour week. Some work evenings and weekends to fit their patients' schedules. About two-thirds of jobs for physical therapists are either in hospitals or in offices of other health practitioners (which includes offices of physical therapists). Other jobs are in home health care services, nursing care facilities, outpatient care centers, and offices of physicians. Some physical therapists are self-employed in private practices, seeing individual patients and contracting to provide services in hospitals, rehabilitation centers, nursing care facilities, home health care agencies, adult day care programs, and schools. Physical therapists also teach in academic institutions and conduct research.

Within the past few years, we have seen greater interest among health care professionals in preventative care. More and more often, physical therapists' services are also being used in a proactive way— to prevent illness and injury. Physical therapists may be hired to evaluate the safety of work sites and home and educational settings, to teach safe work habits, or to design exercise programs. Many companies invest in the safety and wellness of their employees, turning to physical therapists for assistance. Homes and schools with children with disabilities are examined by physical therapists to ensure that the kids are in an optimal and safe environment.

Personal Qualities for Success

As with any profession, there are certain personal qualities, traits, and attributes that you should possess to have success in this field. As you read the following section, critically evaluate whether you possess the described skills, attributes, and interests. If you find yourself able to relate and looking forward to meeting the challenges described, then you very well may be destined for a career in physical therapy.

Physical therapy is a field that provides a service to others. To best provide this service, you will rely on your knowledge of the anatomy, physiology, and human kinetics. Emotionally, you must possess a strong desire to help people. In addition, you must be friendly and genial and genuinely like people from all walks of life. Often, you will have no choice of whom you will or will not treat, and you will interact with people from a range of cultures and with varying levels of education and socioeconomic status. Finally, you must not fear or dislike touching people or being touched because this field requires a great deal of close, personal contact. You will have to use your hands and arms to manipulate people's bodies and to show them the proper way to move. In return, your patients will need to lean on you, to use your strength when theirs is lacking.

Because physical therapy involves serving patients with impaired bodily functions, physical therapists strive to improve their own coordination and sense of rhythm, movement, and balance. Before the therapist can teach correct posture to patients, he or she must possess and practice correct posture. Physical therapy is hard and physically demanding work; most therapists have strong hands, endurance, stamina, and a high energy level. Physical therapists stoop, knead, crouch, and stand for long periods. They also move heavy equipment and lift patients or help them turn, stand, or walk. Historically, most physical therapists were graduates of physical education programs. Although this is no longer a requirement for gaining entry into the field, many practicing physical therapists have had a lifelong interest and experience in a range of athletic activities, including organized or informal sports.

Physical therapy courses are intellectually challenging and require a great deal of motivation and study to complete successfully. Rote memorization of human anatomy and physiology, among other topics, is par for the course. In addition, like all areas of health care, the field is constantly changing and growing. This means that continuing self-education is necessary and, often, mandatory. As in all fields, computer literacy is an advantage both in getting through school and in staying up-to-date after entering the workforce. While your greatest instrument of healing will be your body, the continual evolution of technology in the field requires you to be comfortable with learning and mastering electronic gizmos and gadgets.

Scientific aptitude is essential for success in this field. Several science courses are included in the prerequisites for physical therapy courses, and students have to read a great deal of scientific literature to stay abreast of current trends in health and medicine. To register for physical therapy curricula, most universities require a minimum grade point average ranging from 2.5 to 3.5 (out of 4.0). You can determine whether you possess scientific aptitude by looking at your grades in high school science courses such as biology, chemistry, and physiology. These three courses will be required as prerequisites in college.

Perhaps the most important quality a physical therapist must possess is emotional stability. Because the therapist's life is usually busy to the point of being hectic, and decision-making is a constant and ongoing responsibility, he or she must be able to think and react quickly. There is little or no time for meditation. In addition, you will have to be a multitasker, able to switch gears quickly from patient to patient and able to handle frequent interruptions from other health care staff when you are working with a patient.

Most physical therapists work with patients who are ill; as a result, stressful situations may sometimes occur. Patients receiving physical therapy are generally optimistic and obey directions eagerly to improve their health. Some, however, will have terminal illnesses and may experience one or more of the five stages of grief over dying: denial, anger, bargaining, depression, and acceptance. Because these patients may be difficult to work with, it is especially necessary for the physical therapist to be able to both sympathize and empathize with them. No matter what the patient's situation, many times a physical therapist must prod, encourage, and cajole him or her into completing physical therapy treatments that may be painful.

As with any health care setting in which ill people undergo stressful and strenuous activities, a few patients have died in physical therapy departments. The cause of death is most often cardiac arrest. It is likely that this may occur more frequently as the baby-boom generation continues to mature and more people are living longer lives with concurrent illnesses. This means that physical therapists will treat greater numbers of people with complicated and numerous health concerns. The death of a patient during treatment can be an extremely disturbing experience, and most hospitals or health care settings will have resources available to provide counseling.

Day-to-day care of patients is usually less traumatic, but it certainly has its disagreeable aspects—especially for student therapists and those who are new to the profession. Physical therapists treat patients who have been badly burned, who have deep and odorous ulcers, or who cough and spit up lung secretions. Patients are people who are sick, and they don't stop being sick during their physical therapy sessions. Occasionally, patients will vomit or have bowel or bladder movements during treatment. Then it is necessary for the therapist to help support staff wash the patient and clean the floor.

Tact is an important personality trait for physical therapists to possess. People who are ill and in pain must be dealt with carefully and sensitively. Patients are living individuals who, when you encounter them, will be in a physical and emotional crisis. This means they may be resistant to treatment and may have difficulty understanding the need for particularly painful forms of treatment. You must be able to inspire confidence in them and build a solid working framework with them and their families to provide them with and have them accept the highest-quality care.

Moderate mechanical aptitude is helpful in performing the job to the best of your abilities. Knowing how to handle a screwdriver, a hammer, and a wrench is useful. It isn't necessary to understand all the intricate workings of the machines you use, but you will have to be able to lengthen and shorten crutches and canes. Mechanical ingenuity, the ability to conceive and develop new devices, is a great asset because many physical therapists are called upon to improve and adapt self-help equipment.

Some knowledge of the fundamentals of basic office procedures is also valuable, particularly the principles of budgeting and accounting. This is important because some day you may be promoted to a management position, one that requires running a physical therapy department and staff. Because many physical therapists neglect training in this area, picking up a few basic courses in finance and accounting will give you a leg up on the competition.

Dealing with people demands a good vocabulary and the ability to speak and write clearly. Physical therapists must be adept at directing patients, teaching families, instructing nursing school classes, supervising physical therapy students, reporting on patients' progress to doctors, and demonstrating physical therapy procedures at medical staff conferences. They must be able to write effectively because they may have to prepare clinical notes on patients, annual reports of the department's activities to the hospital board of trustees, and letters to business leaders and prospective employers.

People come in all sizes, shapes, colors, religions, ethnic backgrounds, social levels, and tax brackets. If you cannot deal with people as they are with love, understanding, and total acceptance, physical therapy is not the career for you. Because duties, especially those in the clinical field, involve very close contact with patients, it is necessary that you be willing to have close bodily contact with people, no matter how beautiful or ugly, brilliant or stupid, rich or poor they are. You must also be able to shift your mental gears very quickly because you must adapt to different personalities in rapid succession.

Most physical therapists are of above-average intelligence and are happy, boisterous, athletic, and optimistic people. No rule states that a physical therapist may not be introverted, but because the profession's responsibilities involve people as patients, people as coworkers, and people on the hospital or agency staff, the gregarious individual may find the field more appealing and easier to work in.

As a physical therapist, you must be innovative, looking constantly for improved methods of performance. You must be analytical in order to compare the patient's performance from one day to the next, to compare patients with the same problems, and to determine how new approaches to old problems can be tried. You will need to be courageous. Sometimes it takes courage to convince a physician that a different approach to treatment is worth trying. It will take even more courage to fight a legislative assembly in the state capital or in Washington for the rights you think are legally yours.

Many people believe the pioneer era in our national history has ended. But pioneering still exists, not on the western frontier, but on the frontiers of science. Pioneers on any frontier must possess the same basic characteristics. They must be nonconformists, willing to take criticism for what they believe in. They must have the physical ability to work long hours to achieve their goals. Finally, they must thrive on the adventure of new ideas and opportunities.

If you find that you are able to see many of your qualities and interests in this chapter, and if you are just as excited (or more so) about exploring a career as a physical therapist, then read on!

3

EDUCATION AND TRAINING

RESEARCHING AND APPLYING to schools of higher learning, including community colleges, four-year colleges, and universities, can be a daunting and time-consuming task. However, if you are well informed and organized, it can be accomplished fairly painlessly. While it is beyond the scope of this book to discuss the actual application process—there are many good books that do just that—in this chapter, you will learn about education basics. You will learn how to prepare yourself to be the most appealing college applicant you can be. You will read about what courses of study to expect in both physical therapy and physical therapist assistant programs. And, finally, you will learn about scholarships and grants.

Knowledge is a wonderful thing, and learning about a field as exciting as physical therapy can provide you with immense satisfaction. Enjoy this time and soak up as much information as you can.

Shadowing a Physical Therapist

You can learn a great deal about the history of the field and its philosophical tenets, and get a good sense of the duties of a physical therapist by reading a good book; but observing a physical therapist in action will teach you more than any book can offer. This is true for all fields, not just physical therapy.

Getting a firsthand look at what the work environment is like, what kinds of people work in various settings, how coworkers interact, the typical patient problems a physical therapist treats, and how busy a workday is will give you a true sense of whether this is the kind of job you could happily make your life's work. You can also interview the physical therapist and ask him or her questions about the job, something you could never do with a book. Most people are flattered when others take an interest in their work, and they are usually more than happy to help out by providing their time and expertise. One thing to keep in mind is that because of the HIPAA (Health Insurance Portability and Accountability Act), part of which guarantees patients security and privacy of health information, some hospitals and clinical settings may not allow you to actually shadow a physical therapist as he or she makes the rounds. If you cannot get full access to a physical therapist making rounds, you should still ask for a one-on-one interview.

Getting a Foot in the Door

If you haven't yet obtained the training and education necessary for a job as a physical therapist or therapist assistant, you can still get your foot in the door of a desired place of employment. Temporary employment, volunteering, and working as a nurse's assistant or technician, orderly, or as an administrative assistant will give you entry into a hospital or clinical environment without requiring additional education and training. Not only is this an excellent way to make extra money while completing your education, but you can also build a positive reputation among the staff, giving you a leg up on the competition when it comes time to apply for a physical therapist position.

If you accept a job as a temporary employee, you must work as long as you specified on the application. Leaving early, even if it is for school commitments, will cause a great deal of difficulty for the department; it will be impractical to hire someone for a few weeks, and working short-staffed puts an added strain on all the people you leave. Besides the difficulties you cause, it points out to the director of the department that you lack the maturity and depth for a service career in the health field. The director may never give you another opportunity to work for her or him, nor will that director ever give you a recommendation or reference.

As an aide or orderly, your job will be to transport patients from their rooms to various parts of the hospital or clinic, including the physical therapy department, in wheelchairs or on carts. You will make up treatment tables with fresh linens, empty laundry hampers and sort fresh linen, clean hydrotherapy equipment, and occasionally clean other machines. You may help with clerical work. You will have an opportunity to have direct patient contact by helping the therapists transfer patients from one place to another. Tell the therapists in the physical therapy department that you are interested in the field as a possible career, and they will usually invite you to watch interesting procedures when the work schedule allows it. You can also ask them to explain the importance of procedures and movements as they work. In doing this job, you will be able to see the chain of command in a department, you will learn to talk with patients, and you will become familiar with the types of disabilities that physical therapists handle.

Volunteering in hospitals and clinics is an unpaid position that requires a time commitment of usually two to six hours a week. Depending on the area of need, you may be required to volunteer on weekends or evenings, but you are usually in charge of determining when you will offer your services. Everyone appreciates a volunteer, and this is a great way to show your prospective employer that you care about people and are committed to helping others. Volunteers perform a wide range of services; it's best to contact a hospital or physical therapy center that interests you and inquire about volunteer opportunities. As always, websites are an excellent resource for information, and they usually have a direct link to the volunteer department.

Administrative assistants are the backbone of any organization. They are indispensable resource persons who are unfortunately often overworked and underpaid. That said, being an administrative assistant for a year or two while you are in school is an excellent way to get your foot in the door of the physical therapy department or clinic. You must be adept at handling phones, faxes, and a variety of computer programs, as well as being completely comfortable with handling new technology in this position. You can prove your ability to juggle multiple tasks, meet deadlines, and have meaningful and positive interactions with a wide range of patients in this job.

There are other jobs that bear a connection to the field of physical therapy, albeit a tenuous one. For example, spending the summers working outdoors as a counselor in a camp for disabled children will give you the opportunity to witness, participate in, and organize various fun and educational activities for this specific population. Working as a camp counselor can be an extremely rich and rewarding experience, especially if you think you may someday want to work with children. Oftentimes, this type of job requires no experience beyond being of legal age to work, making this an ideal job for high school students. An online search using appropriate keywords may be your best bet in finding these camps.

Formal Education

Physical therapy is a popular career choice, and competition for admission into physical therapy programs is intense. To gain admission to these programs, students will need good high school and science prerequisite grades and usually some volunteer experience. In addition, many programs require references from employers or former teachers or professors. It is never too early to cultivate good relationships with these people and, before you leave any job or school, be sure to ask your potential referents if they would be willing to provide you with a good reference.

Your education for a career in physical therapy must include a balanced combination of courses that will teach you how to live as well as how to earn a living. You must develop an understanding of humanity's spiritual and social needs as well as our physical requirements. You must learn to think logically, to analyze, and to interpret. You must be able to write and speak effectively. You must learn how to establish good interpersonal relationships. Typical prerequisite or supplemental courses, outside those of your direct field of study, include sociology, psychology, human development across the lifespan, statistics, biology, anatomy and physiology, and chemistry. After you have built this foundation, you can begin planning for your professional courses, which will be discussed in greater detail below. Today's requirements for admission into a physical therapy course are higher than ever before, because scholarship makes the difference between a craft and a profession.

Both physical therapy and physical therapy assistant programs include time spent gaining clinical experience. This begins with a half day per week of observation and expands to working full-time in the final quarter or semester. Students work under the supervision of a therapist, and they apply what they have learned in the academic courses. The clinical rotations include acute hospitals, rehabilitation centers, pediatric and geriatric centers, private practice offices, and homebound work. Some programs assign students to institutions close to the home university. Others, because of their location or the large number of students, must arrange for clinical facilities farther away. Some programs are very strict about the placement of students, while others are more fluid and will attempt to arrange an affiliation in the student's hometown, even though this may not be one of the usual clinical facilities.

As with regular classes on campus, colleges and universities charge a credit hour fee for the period of clinical experience, and students must pay their own transportation from the school to each of two or three facilities and back to the university. In considering the total cost of your education, you must plan for these necessary and inevitable expenses. You will need to purchase two or three uniforms and duty shoes. Good quality uniforms are rather expensive, but they hold their shape longer and are usually more durable. Some schools have their own uniforms or require you to purchase specific ones. Malpractice insurance, even for students, is a necessary expense so that both you and your school are protected in the event that someone is further injured by something you did or did not do.

High School

It bears repeating that it's never too early (or too late!) to lay the groundwork in preparation for entrance into a physical therapy program. High school is the perfect time to learn science basics as well as get the kind of grades that will ensure acceptance into a good program. Your high school education should consist of four years of English, with both speech and journalism courses, if possible. Take two years of a foreign language, two years of mathematics, and one year each of biology, chemistry, physics, history, social science, health, business, and computer science. Spanish is a particularly useful foreign language to take because the number of native Spanish speakers in this country is ever increasing. You should also obtain first aid/CPR certification and keep it up-to-date. There is no age requirement for this type of certification, which is usually offered through the Red Cross, and it is something that would benefit all to learn, so encourage your parents and siblings to get certified with you. Typing is a skill that you will use for the rest of your life, so it's important to take a class to learn how to do it quickly and accurately.

In addition to achieving academically, it's important to show prospective schools that you are a well-rounded individual who is able to participate and excel in a variety of areas. So long as you are not overtaxing yourself, you should participate in activities, clubs, and sports outside the classroom. Being in band, football, volleyball, or the choir, or on the yearbook staff, student council, or honor society will show that you are successful in all areas of life. Participation in sports will also help you learn the fundamentals of movement and the value of exercise.

College or University

No matter what state you currently live in or wish to live in, you are sure to find an accredited physical therapy program near you. According to the American Physical Therapy Association (APTA), as of 2004 there were 209 accredited physical therapy programs offered in the United States. Of these, 111 offered bachelor's degree programs and 98 offered master's degree programs. As of January 1, 2002, the Commission on Accreditation in Physical Therapy Education (CAPTE) no longer accredits baccalaureate professional programs, so this number will continue to decline and the number of master's programs will increase. The reason for this is that the amount of material specific to physical therapy that a student must learn, in addition to prerequisites and required liberal arts classes, is beyond the scope of a baccalaureate program.

There are a variety of different types of programs you can choose from when researching physical therapy educational options. In addition to baccalaureate and master's programs, there are also entry-level doctoral programs and bridge programs for those who have completed schooling as a physical therapist assistant. The latter, however, are rare. If you want to someday practice as a physical therapist, it is not recommended that you seek education as a physical therapist assistant first because the curriculum is significantly different. In other words, you will have to complete (and finance) the full physical therapist program, so being a physical therapist assistant will not provide you with a shortcut to the field.

There are many advantages for the physical therapist with a master's or doctoral degree. When you have had adequate experience, your opportunities for advancement from staff therapist to responsible and interesting positions are numerous. You may be appointed physical therapy educational supervisor in your institution. In this position, you would supervise the clinical students in your institution. You would also arrange and conduct all the in-service programs. You might teach classes of students in the school of nursing or classes of patients. You might even teach interns and residents. You would have the opportunity to advance to the position of assistant director of the department. After this experience, you would be qualified to become the director of a small department, and, later, you would be qualified to assume responsibility for a large department. More and more physical therapists are taking on supervisory roles.

Even as a staff therapist, you would have the authority to evaluate and assess patients. (Physical therapists may not diagnose, so we never use the word *examine*; instead, we use the words *evaluate* or *assess*.) After the evaluation, you would plan the treatment program. You should also consider that as a therapist you would treat patients whose medical problems are more interesting than are those assigned to the assistant. Also, the treatment program is more challenging to your initiative and ingenuity.

There are several factors you should consider and questions you should ask when choosing a physical therapy program. First of all, what is the size of the school and program and where is it located? For some, a large school consisting of a student body of thirty-five thousand and a program size of one thousand offers the appeal of diversity. For others, this would be overwhelming and they may feel lost in the crowd. For the latter, a small campus of only two thousand students, with a program size of fifty would give them the one-on-one kind of attention they desire.

How much is the tuition? State schools are usually less expensive than private schools, and in-state tuition is often significantly less that out-of-state tuition. For example, according to the APTA, total in-state tuition for a baccalaureate degree in physical therapy from a public school was approximately $16,600, for an out-of-state public program it was $39,200, and for a private program it was $52,000. Master's and doctoral degrees are more costly to obtain, but the pay upon graduation will also be incrementally greater. Also, how long is the program? What is the time commitment? This will help you plan ahead. Find out, too, what the licensure pass-rate is and the percentage of students who are employed immediately after graduation. These things will give you a good idea of the quality of the program.

For many master's programs, you will be required to take the Graduate Record Exam (GRE) prior to admission to the program. There are generally two different kinds of GRE tests: the general GRE test and subject-specific GRE tests. The general GRE test can be taken almost any day of the year through a computerized process, and you should have your test scores back in about two weeks. The subject-specific GRE tests are offered in November, December, and April, and those scores are reported some four to six weeks later. Be sure to carefully review the admission guidelines for your program of choice to determine which test may be required. Also, you'll need to be careful of deadlines, both for taking the GRE and for submitting the results to your school. For more information about the GRE, visit its website at http://www.gre.org.

Prior to entry into a program, you must complete the basic prerequisite classes in addition to general classes. These courses include English composition and literature, a foreign language, philosophy, psychology, speech, history, sociology, anthropology, biology, zoology, bacteriology, embryology, chemistry, physics, and mathematics. Be certain that you know what the prerequisites are for admission to the physical therapy curriculum of your choice, as each program has its own requirements. Most schools require a minimum of a 3.0 out of a 4.0 scale in this course work.

In addition to class work in the basic sciences, bachelor's and master's programs include courses in biomechanics, neuroanatomy, human growth and development, manifestations of disease, physical assessment, electrotherapy, research, therapeutic exercise, human anatomy with cadaver dissection, physiology, biophysics, physics, kinesiology, abnormal psychology, medical lectures in many of the specialties, physical therapy procedures, and professional ethics. While you are in college, it will benefit you to take all the physical education courses you can in folk dancing, modern dance, and aerobics. Corrective exercise courses and gymnastics, swimming, and lifesaving are also helpful. If you may choose electives, enroll in courses in educational psychology and methods, because you will be teaching people of all levels of educational achievement throughout your professional life. You may also be teaching in formal classroom situations. Other electives that might be helpful are public speaking, journalism or English, behavioral science, organizational behavior, administration, interpersonal behavior, business or finance, and labor relations. If your computer skills need work, develop them now. Computer science is vital because computers are used for everything, including billing, statistics, and monitoring and recording patient progress.

Appendix A contains a list of accredited physical therapy programs organized by state.

Physical Therapist Assistant

Because the need and demand for physical therapy increased so rapidly after World War II, in 1967 the American Physical Therapy Association established a program for physical therapist assistants. The APTA, which had established the educational requirements for physical therapists, decided upon a degree program that not only gave students both theoretical and practical knowledge, but also stressed the practical application—the how rather than the why. As of 2004 there were 247 accredited physical therapy assistant programs in the United States. The majority of these are associate degree programs, although there are a few baccalaureate programs available.

If you decide to pursue education as a physical therapist assistant, the freshman year curriculum will include many liberal arts courses to provide you with a foundation for intellectual, social, and cultural growth. This background differs from that in a vocational or skill-oriented field. Some schools introduce physical therapy in the freshman year, but others do not offer physical therapy courses until the sophomore year. During the latter part of the course you will spend some time in hospitals, nursing homes, and children's centers to apply what you learned in your classes.

Every job and every level of physical therapy has advantages and disadvantages; that of the physical therapist assistant is no exception. The two-year course is less expensive than the four-year baccalaureate program, and public institutions are more affordable than private institutions. The complete cost of an associate degree in a public institution is approximately $6,500, while that of a private institution is $23,000. Data specific to the baccalaureate programs are hard to track down, but it is likely that the cost of tuition for baccalaureate-prepared physical therapists is similar to that described above. If you are hesitant to take on a sizable loan to finance your education, you can begin working in two years and continue your education by attending evening courses at a nearby college or university. This would enable you to enroll later in a baccalaureate program. Very few community colleges have open-end programs with universities that would allow a graduate with an associate degree to continue in the junior year in a baccalaureate program. Usually, associate degree graduates must take several courses to enter the baccalaureate program and then may have to repeat some of the junior college work, depending upon the requirements of the university they enter.

Many hospitals give employees the fringe benefit of certain professional courses or college credit hours. Also, most universities give free credit hours to members of physical therapy departments where their students are assigned for clinical experience. Depending upon many circumstances, it might be possible for you to receive part of your education free. Remember, these fringe benefits are not routine, nor are they inherent in every job, but they do exist in some places.

Appendix B contains a list of accredited physical therapy assistant programs organized by state.

Scholarships and Financial Aid

Information about scholarships and financial aid is widely available to those willing to search for it. By far the quickest and easiest way to track down information is by using the Internet. Beware of sites that require payment to search for scholarships, as these are disreputable and usually fraudulent sites. Two good sites are FinAid at www.finaid.org and scholarships.com. Typing in keywords such as "physical therapy" and "scholarships" will yield you a plethora of information. Ask your career guidance counselor or the financial aid office at the college of your choice for help in searching. Associations, churches, and professional or military clubs or organizations often offer scholarships to members' children. The APTA offers a booklet—*APTA's Resource Guide on Financial Assistance*—that lists scholarships, fellowships, awards, and grants for physical therapy students. It costs $17 and you can purchase it by calling 800-999-2782, extension 3395. Finally, the government is the biggest lender of money for school. See the U.S. Department of Education website at www.ed.gov for more information.

4

The Nature of the Work

In the previous chapters, you read about the growing need for physical therapists in the health field, and you read what the physical therapist assistant and the physical therapist do, but you didn't read much about how they do these things. At this point, you're probably wondering what a typical day as a physical therapist or therapist assistant is actually like. In this chapter, you will learn all the ins and outs of life as a physical therapist and, by the end of it, you should have a pretty good idea of whether this would be a good career choice for you.

Therapist and Patient

The cornerstone of this job is the relationships and interactions between the physical therapist, the patient, and sometimes the family. After a patient is referred to physical therapy, a physical therapist will evaluate the patient. (Evaluation procedures are described later in the chapter.) All patients treated by physical therapist assistants must first be evaluated by a physical therapist. Furthermore, the physical therapist will perform interim evaluations during the course of the treatment and change the treatment plan if needed. The patient's progress is described in clinical notes, which are written at specified intervals, determined by the hospital or the department policy. These notes are documented proof of treatment, showing what the patient does or does not respond to. Frequently, a therapist will instruct the patient's family in certain procedures to hasten recovery and to prevent further disability, especially in muscles and joints.

The director and the assistant director of the rehabilitation team to which the physical therapist belongs supervise the work of all staff members. These people are often physical therapists holding at least a master's or a doctoral degree. They generally have some form of business or financial experience, either in a previous job or through additional schooling. In some facilities, the director's responsibilities are purely administrative, with no direct patient care. In others, he or she may be treating patients almost eight hours a day, in addition to performing administrative tasks. With this increased workload comes a commensurate level of pay. While at times direct patient service and departmental administration overlap, to show both aspects of the professional obligations more clearly and completely, they have been separated in the explanations that follow.

Some physicians will write "evaluate and treat" orders, allowing the physical therapist to determine the type of treatment most appropriate for the patient's problem. Other doctors choose to write very specific treatment orders, including specifying the number and type of treatments to be given to the patient. In most states not requiring a physician's order, the therapist must have the patient's diagnosis from a physician. As soon as the therapist receives the requisition, he or she learns everything possible about the patient's medical history. If the therapist is not familiar with the diagnosis, he or she will review textbooks for a better understanding of the patient's problems.

If the patient is hospitalized, the therapist must decide whether it is better to administer treatment in the physical therapy department or at the bedside. Usually, the only patients who receive treatments at the bedside are those who cannot be moved safely from their beds. Whenever possible, therapists bring their patients to the department because the facilities there are better equipped, they can spend more time with the patients, the change of scenery is stimulating, and the other patients present offer a great deal of encouragement.

Aides and orderlies transfer patients from beds to carts or wheelchairs and then transport the patients to the department. They also assist the patients in getting onto the treatment tables and in preparing them for the treatments. Physical therapist assistants will often take over for the aides or orderlies once they arrive at the physical therapy department.

Physical therapist assistants perform components of physical therapy procedures and related tasks selected by a supervising physical therapist. In a given day, physical therapist assistants undertake a variety of tasks. Components of treatment procedures performed under the direction and supervision of physical therapists involve exercises, massages, electrical stimulation, paraffin baths, hot and cold packs, traction, and ultrasound. Physical therapist assistants record the patient's responses to treatment and report the outcome of each treatment to the physical therapist.

Before a therapist begins any test or treatment, the patient's confidence must be won. This is a simple matter with intelligent and cooperative adults, but it is much more difficult with frightened children. In handling children, it is often necessary to spend as much time in the emotional preparation for treatment as in the actual treatment. Children who have experienced pain with previous treatments often have difficulty understanding that the pain is something they must continue to work through to get better. With adults, the therapist must explain what is to be done, why it is necessary, and what will be gained from it. He or she must involve the patient in the treatment plan and give the patient options or choices, such as which exercise to accomplish first, to allow them to feel more in charge of their care. Allowing for a period of reflection after treatment will further engage the patient in his or her own care, which is necessary to achieve compliance.

Patient Evaluation

After establishing a working friendship, the therapist is ready to evaluate the patient. This may be a complex and time-consuming procedure that may help in the diagnosis of a baffling problem. More frequently, however, it is a relatively simple assessment of the patient's abilities and limitations when a diagnosis is already made and verified. Evaluation involves using most of your senses as you talk with patients. You will observe them, ask questions, listen to them, touch them, and—this may be a bit surprising to you now— smell them. (A person with uncontrolled diabetes will have an unmistakably fruity smell to their breath.)

Types of Diagnostic Tests

Physical therapists perform four types of diagnostic tests: electrical muscle testing, test of voluntary muscle power, joint measurement, and functional activity tests. If a patient is paralyzed without any apparent reason, the physical therapist may perform tests with electrical currents to determine whether the damage is to the brain, the spinal cord, the nerves carrying the impulse from the spinal cord to the muscle, or to the muscle itself. Where physical therapists once relied on X-rays to gather information, they now use computed tomography (CT scans) to get a better image of a patient's body. Computed tomography is used in many situations to visualize various internal organs and tissues. For example, it helps diagnose and treat patients with spinal stenosis—pain in the lower extremities caused by degenerative diseases that affect the joints.

One test for muscle function is the electromyographic test, which measures muscle response and nerve conduction. A doctor or a specially trained therapist inserts a needle into a muscle or an electrode over a muscle on the surface of the skin. When the muscle contracts, it sends out electrical impulses that travel from the muscle through the needle and wires to a writing apparatus called an oscilloscope or to a computer video monitor. The doctor reads the graph and learns a great deal about the condition of the muscle from the pattern of the electrical waves shown on it. Computer analysis assesses the test results. An advanced technique in this area is called single-fiber electromyography, which measures individual muscle fiber movement. Not only does electromyography aid in diagnosis, but it also provides information about disease processes that may be useful in planning therapy.

In another group of electrical tests, the therapist places an active electrode fastened to a pencil-like applicator on the myoneural junction or motor point, the place where the nerve enters the muscle. By observing whether the muscle responds, how it responds, and the amount of time necessary for the contraction, the therapist can determine whether there is damage to the brain, to the peripheral nerve trunks, or to the muscles. After repeated tests, the therapist knows whether a nerve is healing or dying. This description is, of course, an oversimplification of a difficult and time-consuming procedure.

The most common test of a patient's ability to move is the manual muscle test, or the test of voluntary muscle power. Manual muscle testing requires patience, practice, and experience, as well as a thorough knowledge of muscle function and substitute motions. In this test, when the patient attempts to perform a certain movement, the therapist observes whether the muscle can take normal resistance to the motion, move the part against gravity, move the part with gravity eliminated, or contract the muscle only without producing any movement. The patient repeats the motion several times so that the therapist can observe the endurance of the muscles.

Muscles can contract strongly and permanently in cases of damage to certain areas of the brain or spinal cord or with severe disuse. If a muscle is not able to relax when the opposite muscle contracts, the condition is called *spasticity*. In testing for a spastic muscle, the therapist moves the muscle through the motion to observe whether the muscle jerks, remains contracted, or relaxes. A combination of exercises and medications will help treat spasticity.

Muscle testing in the legs usually includes gait analysis. By observing alignment of a patient's bones, in standing and walking, a therapist can confirm findings in other tests for weakness and spasticity. The position of the weak and spastic muscles, the areas of weight bearing in the feet, and the manner in which a patient walks all combine to help the doctor and the therapist decide whether a patient needs braces, lifts, or specific exercises. It also helps the physical therapist know exactly what areas of the body are not functioning properly. There is specially designed equipment available that electronically measures the gait strength or how hard the foot strikes the floor.

Testing procedures are not limited to specific muscles. Many patients receiving physical therapy suffer from brain damage at birth or in old age. These people may have lost their ability to move, their sensation, or their sense of position. Some may have lost part of their vision, while others lose their hearing, and a few lose both. Many older adults who are paralyzed on the side of the dominant hand lose their speech or their understanding of words. Before therapists can begin a program to restore function in the affected arm and leg, they must know the extent of the brain damage. They learn this by observing the patient's performance.

Goniometry is the measurement of joint motion. This is another important part of the testing procedure. The therapist uses a goniometer to measure how many degrees a joint moves. This instrument is most commonly and inexpensively an adaptation of the common protractor, but a high-tech version can also be purchased that measures and records multiple joint angles at once. This measurement is compared to the standard degree of movement for a noninjured joint. The therapist repeats the measurement at regular intervals to gauge how rapidly the patient is recovering function—or possibly to conclude that the patient won't recover any motion at all in the joint.

Activities of Daily Living (ADL)

Besides determining the source and extent of paralysis and the limitation of joint motion, the therapist must also know how well a patient can function with whatever motion is left after a disease or injury. The therapist tests the performance of activities of daily living by observing how patients feed, bathe, and dress themselves; how they write or use a computer, handle a telephone, and maneuver a wheelchair. This helps to assess whether the patient will require additional help when he or she returns home, either in the form of personnel or equipment. These patients may also require additional information on making their home environments safer and more compatible to living with their injuries.

Scientific Research in Movement

Every year scientists continue to learn more about how the human body works, and their research is often directly translated into practical applications within the field of physical therapy. Scientific groups around the world have long been studying reflexes and the normal progression of motor skills in infants and young children. Through their research, physicians and physical therapists have learned that:

1. Certain sensations, such as cold, tapping, brushing, or rubbing will cause a muscle to contract when the usual progression of the conventional exercise program fails to produce motion.
2. Adults and children learn to walk more easily if they have learned to do all the things that normal infants and children do before walking. If a patient can roll over, crouch, crawl, and kneel upright, walking is less difficult.
3. Motor reflexes, certain involuntary movements over which a patient at first has no control, can be used as a foundation for teaching willed and voluntary motion.

Five systems of exercise have developed using these basic neurological and developmental principles. Each system is different from the others in its approach to treating the patient. Some therapists use one system exclusively; others take parts from all the systems to achieve results.

For anyone interested in research, investigation into the vast field of motor development would be a challenging and intellectually stimulating field to enter. Most master's and doctoral programs require students to conduct research, so you will likely get a sense of it during college. You may find that you have a knack for applying the scientific process and decide to pursue a career in research rather than in direct patient care. Research is instrumental in helping physical therapists decide how to treat patients and product developers create new and better tools and instruments.

Exercise Programs

After determining the extent of a disability, the therapist plans an exercise program to build the patient's strength and increase the range of motion of his or her muscles. Planning such a program to restore the patient to a productive life is the most stimulating and rewarding responsibility of a physical therapist. In addition to being an educator, the physical therapist is also a coach and cheerleader when performing this part of the job.

Traditional Therapeutic Program

Exercise undertaken in a therapeutic exercise program is much different from the calisthenics performed in a typical physical education class. Sometimes treatment begins with passive motion, in which the therapist moves a body part for the patient to make the patient aware of the sensation of motion. Knowledge of the sensation is fundamental to all voluntary movement. The next step is passive assistive motion, in which the therapist moves the body part, with the patient helping a little. The third step is active assistance exercise, in which the patient moves, with the therapist offering some assistance. Next, the patient moves without any assistance. Last, the patient moves against resistance offered by a therapist or by weights attached to the arms or legs. Those who have practiced weight lifting know that muscles gain strength more quickly when they move against resistance than by moving more frequently without resistance. This pattern of exercise has been the conventional and traditional program for nearly as long as the profession has been recognized in the United States.

Evidence-Based Therapeutic Programs

Using evidence from research acquired over time, the field of physical therapy has developed and continues to refine therapeutic treatment programs for patients experiencing a variety of problems, injuries, disabilities, or diseases. This section describes some of the many treatments in use today. While this section is by no means exhaustive, it should give you a good idea of the variety of ways you can treat patients.

In general hospitals, therapists frequently teach patients to walk with crutches, without placing any weight on an injured leg or by placing partial weight on a weak or painful leg. The therapist must fit the crutches to the patient and decide which of the five crutch gaits is best for that patient. As soon as the patient can walk independently, the therapist will instruct the patient how to sit down, rise from a chair, and climb and descend stairs. Not all patients can use crutches; some never pass beyond the walker stage, while others advance quickly to a cane. Sometimes after a patient learns to walk, a therapist may teach her or him to run, skip, and perform some ballroom, folk, and modern dance movements.

Physical therapists also assist with treatment of lung diseases. Physical therapists have long been aware of the value of pulmonary care for patients suffering from lung congestion. In this exercise system, the patient lies in a certain position to drain the fluid from a specific lobe of the lung. While the patient is tilted, the therapist claps and vibrates (two massage techniques) over the lobe being drained. The patients also learn breathing exercises that emphasize breathing out and coughing.

Many obstetrical patients learn groups of abdominal exercises before and after the delivery of a baby. Sometimes the therapist teaches these in classes, but more frequently he or she instructs each patient independently. This helps the patient strengthen muscles that will help deliver the baby. Many of these techniques have crossed over to birthing classes that many couples take prior to delivery of their baby.

In nearly every hospital, it is common practice for therapists to teach posture correction exercises to patients who have pain resulting from poor body mechanics and to youngsters who are developing bad postural habits that might produce serious deformities. Scoliosis or curvature of the spine is a fairly common problem that is often diagnosed in childhood or adolescence. For those with scoliosis, good body mechanics, including correcting posture and strengthening back and abdominal muscles, is necessary to prevent further twisting of the spine.

Orthopedic physical therapy is a rapidly expanding specialty. Therapists who use this treatment must learn the techniques of mobilization and manipulation used in osteopathy. The therapists who use mobilization and manipulation of joints to increase the range of motion must take many advanced courses, and they must continue to study independently and to practice constantly. This therapy requires specialized techniques and knowledge as well as special skill in working with the patients to create an atmosphere conducive to their complete cooperation and relaxation during the procedures. Manual therapy, as it is called in physical therapy, can increase range and relieve pain dramatically and rapidly, in the situations where it is indicated. Although many therapists have learned to mobilize, some have had difficulty in timing the manipulation thrust. Another technique in the same category is a form of osteopathy known as "strain and counter strain," which combines pressure with position to relieve pain.

Craniosacral therapy (CST) is another osteopathic technique to relieve pain. It, too, requires intensive postgraduate studies. CST is a relatively new form of therapy that was developed in the mid-1970s to the mid-1980s. It is mostly used as a preventive health measure to bolster the body's resistance to disease and to diminish pain and dysfunction associated with the central nervous system. In CST, the practitioner uses gentle pressure to, in effect, massage areas of the head and spine. The intent is to release restrictions of the cerebrospinal fluid in the head and spine.

Every physical therapy department has exercise equipment that a patient may use independently before or after a session with the therapist. The weights, wands, stall bars, wrist rolls, shoulder wheels, pulleys, and bicycles all emphasize the need for the patient to assume the responsibility for her or his own exercise program. The patient must not depend totally upon the therapist for improvement. Sometimes yoga and Pilates positions and dance patterns are included in the exercise program.

A physical therapist uses different exercises for different disabilities, but exercises are beneficial for many conditions, including polio, cerebral palsy, hemiplegia, spinal cord injury, multiple sclerosis, muscular dystrophy, Parkinson's disease, emphysema, bronchiectasis, cystic fibrosis, arthritis, burns, nerve and muscle lacerations, poor posture, mental illness, and the postoperative care of amputees. Patients who have had corrective bone, joint, and muscle surgery also use these exercises.

Often the exercise program begins in a pool or in a large tank of water. The buoyancy of the water makes movement easier, and a weak muscle can develop strength and coordination more rapidly. Sometimes patients begin walking in pools or in specially designed tanks. Water also helps offset the effects of gravity, which makes an enormous difference to patients whose muscles have atrophied or wasted away.

The Modalities

A word used frequently in physical therapy jargon is *modalities*. Physical therapists use this word to refer to a method of therapy that involves physical or electrical therapeutic treatment. Physical treatment includes light, water, temperature, and sound. Some school faculty members and professional leaders prefer not to use this term because its definition varies amongst fields of study, but clinicians working in the field continue to use it. Essentially, the modalities in physical therapy are standard treatment methods, some of which we touched on in earlier chapters. In this section, we will explore the various methods of treatment used by the physical therapist and the physical therapist assistant. In most cases, the physical therapist assistant may perform the modalities described here. In fact, on a day-to-day basis, the assistant's activities and responsibilities include many of these treatment procedures; if a department has no assistant, the physical therapist will administer them.

Hydrotherapy

Hydrotherapy is the use of water in treatment. The water is usually warm and slightly above body temperature. The water is caused to whirl by a jet of air forced from a turbine that looks like an outboard motor but that, of course, has no rotor blades. Immediately following severe trauma (accident), patients, including athletes involved in sports-related injuries, are typically treated in very cold water. Another form of hydrotherapy, the contrast bath, is a popular and easy form of home treatment that therapists often teach patients suffering from arthritis of the hands and feet. The contrast bath alternates between hot and cold water in a specific time sequence.

The combination of heat and the water massage helps to relieve pain and to increase circulation. It is also beneficial in cleansing an arm or leg after a cast, splint, or dressing has been removed or when a large area of tissue has been severely burned, frostbitten, or ulcerated.

Paraffin Baths

Paraffin baths—the use of paraffin and mineral oil mixed together and heated to temperatures between 123 and 132 degrees Fahrenheit—provide an effective relief from the pain of arthritis and inflammation of the tendons of the hands and feet. They are also one of the mainstays of physical therapy treatment for patients who suffer from leprosy. The patient simply dips her or his hands into the wax about seven times, then continues to soak the hands in the wax or wraps the paraffin-coated hands in a towel for twenty to thirty minutes. Paraffin baths can be purchased for home use as well.

Hot Packs

Hot packs—pads containing a mixture of silicon, gelatin, and chemicals—retain heat for relatively long periods of time and effectively reduce pain. A thermostatically controlled cabinet keeps the packs hot until the therapist wraps them in towels and applies them to a patient. Elastogel Packs can be heated in an oven or microwave or frozen in a freezer as a convenient method of conductive heat or cold. Some of these packs are even scented for additional relaxation effects. Simply opening the wrappers of some over-the-counter packs that can be purchased in your drugstore will activate the heating action.

Radiant Heat

Heat from an infrared lamp often precedes other procedures such as massage or exercise. Both infrared and ultraviolet rays are forms of radiant heat, but they are at opposite ends of the color spectrum, so the effects are totally different. Ultraviolet produces no heat but has instead a chemical effect upon the skin. The patient notices a mild sunburn several hours after the exposure, just as you notice a sunburn after you return from the beach. Ultraviolet is successful in the treatment of skin diseases and is especially beneficial in promoting the healing of pressure sores.

Diathermy

Diathermy is a form of heat produced by the resistance of the tissues to the short waves of an electrical current. Because the heat is a milder dosage of the same inductotherm used to melt metal in the steel mills, the diathermy cannot be used on patients who have metal implanted in their bones. Diathermy that penetrates from one-and-a-half to two inches brings great comfort to patients with aches and pains in muscles and joints.

Ultrasound

Ultrasound has proven to be an extremely effective measure in reducing pain, especially after sudden injuries such as sprains and strains. There are many other conditions that respond to sound, such as arthritis, bursitis, tendinitis, and muscular pains. More recently, sound has been successful in the treatment of warts on the sole of the foot and around the nail beds of fingers and toes.

Ultrasound waves are faster than waves in the range of human hearing. Ultrasound is produced by a current of electricity passing through a transducer that has a round-headed probe. The physical therapist applies ultrasound by moving the probe over the painful area. High-frequency sound waves travel deep into body tissues creating heat. Hands and feet, which have irregular contours, may be treated underwater or the skin may be covered with a gel that makes for a smoother surface.

Electrical Current

You read earlier of the use of electrical current in testing muscles and nerves. These currents are also used in treatment. In one type of treatment, called iontophoresis or ion transfer, the current deposits chemicals or medicines on wounds or ulcers to hasten healing. This is a painless procedure. In addition to distributing medication, the electrical current used to stimulate muscle contractions teaches the muscle to move again when it has forgotten how or when it is too weak to move voluntarily.

Direct current, called *galvanic current*, has been successful in reducing pain. For many years, this style of high voltage treatment was in vogue, but since 1985, the application of micro-amperage currents proved to be more successful in sports medicine and other types of trauma, as well as podiatry.

Transcutaneous Electrical Nerve Stimulation (TENS)

TENS, as the name implies, is used to simulate nerves, muscles, and cells via the skin's surface. TENS, a low-volt galvanic application, is a battery-operated device with electrodes placed upon the patient in the area of pain, or on the acupoints applicable to the pain. Electrodes conduct low-level electrical currents that prompt the brain to produce endorphins that help relieve pain. TENS units are worn by patients who suffer from constant, chronic pain. Therapists instruct the patient in the points of application and periods of time to be used to obtain relief from pain. This is primarily a home care modality and rarely used in a clinical setting, except for testing its efficacy and for instruction.

Ice

During World War II, when physical therapy began to gain momentum, almost every treatment order read, "heat, massage, and exercise." Today, ice is an effective method of reducing pain and spasticity. Patients experience almost immediate relief from pain and an increase in their range of motion. This is because ice application slows the inflammation and swelling that occur after injury. Most pain is accompanied by some type of inflammation, and addressing the inflammation helps reduce the pain. Ice massage therapy also numbs sore tissues (providing pain relief like a local anesthetic); slows the nerve impulses in the area, which interrupts the pain-spasm reaction between the nerves; and decreases tissue damage.

The therapist may apply crushed ice in a plastic or rubber bag to a specific area or he or she may massage the wrapped ice over several muscles and tissues. Usually the patient receives additional instruction in the use of ice at home. Patients who are spastic because they suffer from multiple sclerosis are often submerged in a tub of ice water for four minutes, and this cold-water treatment relieves the spasticity for many hours.

Traction

Many patients who suffer from pain in the low back, neck, or head receive relief from traction. The traction can be steady or intermittent. The patient may be lying down or sitting up. The traction can be applied to the lower back or to the neck with a pelvic belt or a head halter. Traction will stretch the muscles and increase circulation and often results in the correction of joint dysfunction.

Vasopneumatic Compression Devices

Some patients have a great deal of swelling in their arms and legs from a variety of causes. They are helped by means of a vasopneumatic compression device, which forces the fluid from the extremities by pressure within a sleeve or stocking. The treatments last for varying periods of time, ranging from three to twenty-four hours a day. When the edema or swelling has gone, the therapist measures the arm or leg with special tapes, at points an inch and a half apart, for custom-made, pressure-gradient supports to give the circulatory system some help.

Massage

For centuries, in all parts of the world, massage has been a method of relieving pain, inducing relaxation, and increasing circulation. Physical therapists massage to increase circulation, to relieve pain, and to stretch tight muscles. In more recent years, stretching of the fascia has become an important method of relieving areas of tissue tension. This is called *myofascial release*; it can be a very painful procedure, but it is extremely effective. Currently, therapists use massage techniques in the treatment of specific muscular or fascial problems. It is rare for a physical therapist to administer a complete body massage for relaxation.

Acu-Therapy

The Chinese began developing acupuncture treatments four thousand years ago by inserting needles into various parts of the body. The Japanese used the same concept, but they applied pressure instead of needles and called it Shiatsu. Western allopathic medicine has looked askance at this therapy for many decades, but research is recognizing that 70 percent of the acupoints are the myoneural junctions. There has been shown to be a relationship between the acupoints and the body's electrophysiology, and the release of the endorphins and enkephalins in the brain.

The philosophy behind this form of treatment is much too complicated to detail here, but in the practice of acu-therapy, physical therapists apply an electrical current or pressure, a cold laser, or a cold spray to the acupoints. In the United States, physical therapists may not insert needles, although this is permitted in other countries. In the United States, physical therapists use acu-therapy primarily for pain relief.

Therapists interested in this approach to treating pain must attend continuing education courses, because it is not a part of the curriculum in general academic courses.

Many Other Duties

During a typical day, a therapist or an assistant will do many more things than those just described. You may consult with a physician to decide the best type of brace for a patient or the height of a lift on a shoe. You might teach a patient how to put on an artificial arm or leg and how to use the prosthesis effectively. You might put dressings over wounds. In some hospitals with burn units, physical therapists debride necrotic tissue—that is, they scrub, scrape, and cut away skin so badly burned that it is dead. Finally, you may saw off canes, take photographs of unusual conditions, make splints out of plaster of paris or other materials, and make permanent records of deformities of hands and feet by using finger paint and felt marking pens.

The Physical Therapist as an Administrator

In the early years of physical therapy, the therapist, like the doctor of earlier times, had a one-on-one relationship with patients. It was the great personal contact of "laying on of hands" and the resulting gratitude from patients that brought many people into the field in its earlier days. Today the average physical therapist in the United

States works with a team of professionals: physicians, dentists, nurses, occupational therapists, speech-language pathologists, and audiologists. In addition, the physical therapist must spend a great amount of time providing written documentation of the patient's plan of care. The comparatively rapid shift from the therapist's responsibility for the total care of the patient to the current role of administrator and teacher has resulted from the population explosion, the increased public demands for better health care, and expanded physical therapy treatments.

The Department Director

The director of a department is a position that demands great professional and personal dedication. Directors are very special kinds of leaders. They have two responsibilities: one to the hospital administration and one to their own staffs. But they must be primarily concerned with the development of the staff and with the constant improvement of the department's service.

Department directors often play many roles. They are guides, planners, overseers, evaluators, interpreters, reporters, teachers, and, sometimes, counselors, confessors, and peacemakers. In each role, they are expected to excel!

The concrete and tangible responsibilities of those in this position are many and varied. They may assist in designing a desirable floor plan for a new department or decide on the new equipment that the hospital or center requires to meet the needs of the community. Department directors cooperate with the administration, the controller, and the accounting departments in establishing a budget and working within that budget. They assist in setting an equitable fee scale based on actual cost. They assist in preparing forms for referrals, records, billing, and inventory. They also prepare statistics and periodic reports of department activity. The director or chief therapist will attend medical staff meetings where physical therapy patients are discussed and will review patients' progress for the doctors. In some hospitals, the director accompanies the doctors on ward rounds.

Directors work closely with the personnel department to prepare job descriptions, personnel policies, and a just salary scale. They help to recruit and select the staff. The search for a professional physical therapy staff is relentless, because the current competition for new graduates is high. The pressure of offering continuing education opportunities and maintaining morale is constant because the turnover is steady no matter how ideal the working conditions.

Department directors represent the hospital administration to the physical therapy department staff and the staff to the administration. Directors attend department head meetings and relay the important information learned there. They must always insist that their staff comply with all the hospital or institution rules. On the other hand, they have an obligation to their employees to communicate problems to the administration and to back just demands. This may sound as though department heads are walking a tightrope—and it often seems that way!

Teaching and Student Supervision

Often a director of physical therapy may serve in any number of teaching positions. If a hospital has a school of nursing, the director of physical therapy may serve as a guest lecturer in such areas as body mechanics, transfer techniques, massage, crutch walking, orthopedics, and the care of the patient who has had a stroke. In a hospital or rehabilitation center serving as an affiliating center for physical therapy students in the final phase of their professional education, the department director, assistant director, or clinical supervisor oversees the students' clinical experience; critiques, counsels, and consoles them; and prepares extensive reports on their performances. As a member of the clinical faculty of a physical therapy school, the director or a delegate will attend many of the regular faculty meetings.

The duties of the director also vary depending on the size of the organization for which he or she works. In large departments, where the staff may include as many as twenty-five professional physical therapists and a greater number of subprofessional and nonprofessional workers, the director will serve only as an administrator and coordinator. The director will give no individual patient treatment and will probably designate a qualified staff member to be responsible for teaching programs. In medium-sized departments, the director may or may not give treatment, may perform only tests and certain evaluative procedures, or treat very difficult patients. In a private practice, or in a small department, the director may be the one-person show, administering all treatments.

5

PLACES OF EMPLOYMENT

WHEN YOU BEGIN the professional practice of physical therapy, your responsibility will be to the patient as a whole, not to the specific body part in question. You must treat the entire person—the mind and social behavior—as well as the body to ensure complete treatment and healing. However, there are many areas of specialty within physical therapy because there are many different kinds of patients and patient needs. There are also many different kinds of work you might do and various places of employment where you might work. It is beyond the scope of this book to tell you about every type of hospital, institution, agency, and specialty where physical therapists work. In this chapter, the larger areas of employment opportunities will be described.

Where Physical Therapy Happens

Two-thirds of physical therapists and three-fourths of physical therapist assistants work in hospitals or physical therapy offices. In most hospitals the care is centered on patients with acute diseases and disabilities. Some of these patients are admitted primarily for physical therapy and rehabilitation procedures, while others are admitted for medical or surgical care but receive physical therapy as an additional aid to recovery. Many patients are outpatients in hospital departments or private practice offices. Nursing homes and rehabilitation centers employ physical therapists. Patients who live at home, but who are too infirm to be transported, are sometimes treated in their homes. Schools or school districts must also employ physical therapists. Sports medicine and industrial clinics are areas that are increasingly in demand.

Hospital Setting

As previously mentioned, the majority of physical therapists and assistants work in hospitals. Hospitals in big cities usually have large, well-equipped departments while those in less-populated areas have small physical therapy offices. Therapists who work in smaller hospitals are more likely to practice at the bedside than those who work in larger hospitals.

A medical director often heads physical therapy departments. The medical director might be a physiatrist (a doctor specializing in physical medicine and rehabilitation) who is on duty in the department full-time to examine all new patients, to prescribe and observe treatment and the patient's reaction to it, to change orders of other physicians, and to recommend specific types of braces and artificial limbs. There are relatively few physiatrists in our country. Except for a very few hospitals where a physiatrist is on duty all day, the working director is the physical therapist in charge of the department. This therapist might be called "director" or "supervisor" or "chief" depending on the hospital, but whatever the title, her or his responsibilities are the same—operating an efficient department that gives every patient the best possible care.

In some larger, more progressive hospitals, there has been a trend toward the establishment of a committee or board to serve as the medical consultant team. This board is usually composed of an orthopedist, a neurologist, an internist, a rheumatologist, a psychiatrist, and, if possible, a specialist in respiratory disease. The committee meets regularly with the physical therapy director to review administrative, medical, and legal problems.

Very large departments may have as many as thirty or thirty-five physical therapists and physical therapist assistants, while a small department may have only the chief physical therapist and one assistant. There will also be nonprofessional aides and orderlies who transport patients, make beds, sort linen, clean equipment, and fill hydrotherapy tanks. All large departments have clerk-receptionists who receive patients and direct them to the proper areas, pay and type up bills, answer the phone, deliver messages, type routine letters and reports, and file.

In small hospitals the medical director may be an orthopedist, internist, or general practitioner serving without salary on an on-call basis. He or she may give very little supervision to the physical therapy staff and be called only in a crisis. In such a department, the chief therapist is responsible for all direct patient care and all administrative details. The small department may or may not have paraprofessional, nonprofessional, and clerical staff.

The larger physical therapy departments usually have a reception room, an office, and an electrotherapy area where patients receive treatments such as diathermy, ultrasound, infrared, ultraviolet, hot packs, ice, electrical stimulation, paraffin, traction, massage, and some of the exercise programs. In the hydrotherapy area there may be a pool or a Hubbard tank where patients lie for underwater exercises. There are usually a number of smaller whirlpools also. The gymnasium, or exercise room, has a set of parallel bars, walkers, and crutches, canes, and practice staircases for walking training. Often there are stall bars, shoulder wheels, pulleys, wrist rolls, finger ladders, wands, weights, bicycles, floor mats, and other exercise equipment.

Many small departments consist of only one room, with one machine of each type in it, as well as the gait-training equipment and office furniture. In such a small department, every inch of space must be used to maximum efficiency.

Depending upon where your hospital is located, as a physical therapist, you may end up treating a variety of different problems or the same kind of problem repeatedly. Although the patients in general hospitals experience a variety of difficulties, those receiving physical therapy usually suffer from the same problems of arthritis, strokes, fractures, lacerations, ruptured discs, and other back and posture-related difficulties. In some of the larger metropolitan hospitals with many specialists, the physical therapist may treat patients with the more rare neuromuscular diseases such as multiple sclerosis, muscular dystrophy, transverse myelitis, Guillain-Barre syndrome, Parkinson's disease, and post-polio syndrome. Physical therapy also is used for patients suffering from lung diseases such as asthma and its complications, pneumonia, cystic fibrosis (a disease that affects many parts of the body, but especially the lungs), and many others. Physical therapists can help these patients by instructing them in pulmonary exercises and by performing postural drainage.

There are other health issues physical therapists deal with that are less commonly known. In centers where there is a great deal of heart surgery performed, or where there is a cardiac care unit, the physical therapist may develop an exercise program to increase strength and endurance and to increase the amount of air the patient can inhale and exhale. Following surgery, a patient is instructed in exercises to correct posture and to increase shoulder motion. Some skin problems, such as ulcers and burns, are treated with whirlpool, iontophoresis, hyperbaric oxygen, and ultraviolet light. Involvement of physical therapists in obstetrics and gynecology will vary with the interest of the doctors in certain types of problems, use of natural childbirth, and postdelivery rehabilitation. In some institutions the physical therapist works with the orthodontist on problems of the temporal mandibular joint, in facial exercises, and in correcting postural problems that are now recognized to be concurrent with some dental problems. In some hospitals, physical therapists as well as occupational therapists treat patients in psychiatric wards.

Each hospital and department has a personality of its own. In big cities, where the crime rate is high, many gunshot and stab wound patients may receive intensive physical therapy during the rehabilitation period. In large industrial communities, the number of trauma patients from job-related injuries can be high. Many of these patients have fractures from falls, brain damage from blows to the head, and severe lacerations from machinery. Hospitals in mining communities also treat large numbers of industrial accident cases that occur in the mines. In farming communities, hand injuries result from accidents that occur while people are feeding animals or repairing farm machinery. In sheep and cattle country, sheepherders and ranchers suffer from fractures and ruptured spinal discs from falling off horses, especially before and during rodeo season. Burns are common in areas where there are foundries and steel mills. In ski resorts there are many people with fractured legs. In the retirement areas of Florida and Arizona there are many older patients with strokes and arthritis.

Education, experimentation, and research are also par for the course for physical therapists and assistants working in hospitals. In large hospitals, therapists have an excellent opportunity to attend medical staff conferences, special medical seminars, and ward rounds. They may also participate in experiments and research. Usually physical therapy students obtain their clinical experience in the larger, better-equipped hospitals in more cosmopolitan centers, so the staff in these hospitals can participate in their training program.

Smaller hospitals tend to have fewer educational and research opportunities for physical therapists. Therapists in small departments, in small hospitals, and in small towns see fewer rare diseases, have less opportunity to share in medical education, and have fewer opportunities to teach. They may need to possess more imagination and initiative to achieve fulfillment or they may appreciate the slower pace of things. A therapist in a small hospital may have to convert an area never intended for physical therapy into an efficient department. He or she will function with very little medical supervision. One rewarding difference, however, is that in a small hospital, there tends to be a much closer relationship and level of camaraderie between all personnel.

Pediatrics

While every child thrives on love, nurturing, and care, the disabled child needs more than the expression of love through tender words and cuddling. He or she needs the expression of love through deeds. There is nothing more gratifying to a physical therapist than the knowledge that, through his or her efforts, a disabled child has learned to cope better with life's problems. Perhaps this is the reason why almost every physical therapy student expresses a desire to work with children, for at least a short period.

Some large cities and some smaller cities with large medical school complexes have general hospitals exclusively for children. The children may be as young as newborns or as old as sixteen or seventeen. They may have acute diseases or they may have chronic conditions requiring reconstructive procedures. Only a small percentage of the children in these hospitals require physical therapy. Many of the children receiving physical therapy in the hospitals for the acutely ill suffer from cystic fibrosis, or they receive preoperative and postoperative care when surgery to the muscles, tendons, joints, or nerves will make motion easier and more effective.

Children's hospitals offer both long- and short-term care for those requiring some form of physical therapy. Most children's hospitals offer programs of extended convalescent care or prolonged "habilitation" programs. The children remain in the hospital from several weeks to several years. There are usually school programs, scout troops, and other organized social activities within the hospital. About 25 percent of all orthopedically disabled children require a period of hospitalization, and one-third of these live in rural areas where there are no facilities for medical care. For this reason, rural children must remain hospitalized for longer periods than children in large cities, who may report for treatment to hospitals or private offices or may receive treatment in school.

The furniture and treatment equipment in children's hospitals are child size to accommodate the patient population. Instead of walkers, the children sometimes use weighted doll buggies, which engages them in treatment. Other children develop their walking skills by using skis equipped with high poles to hold. The therapist frequently treats children on a mat on the floor rather than on a high treatment table because it is less intimidating for the child. There is also a great deal of pool work to encourage general and specific motions.

If you were working in a children's hospital, you would discuss your treatment objectives with the nurses in each ward, so that the treatment plan would be reinforced in playtime and in school sessions. You would also work closely with the occupational and speech therapists to coordinate and intensify each treatment program. When a child was ready for discharge, you would give the parents detailed instructions in the necessary exercises that they would continue at home.

Public Schools

There are several different ways in which physical therapists work in the school system. Some metropolitan areas have special schools with specific equipment for disabled children; smaller communities may have one classroom housed in a regular school building. Physical therapists sometimes visit several schools to treat these children.

Unlike children's hospitals, the main purpose of the school for the disabled child is education. It is not primarily a treatment center with a school program added. While the treatment program in the school is important, it is secondary to the academic program.

The same basic principles of education that are involved in teaching academic subjects apply to the teaching of a motor activity. Motivation is basic to all treatment, and the treatment must be planned to develop the child's will to improve. The physical therapist must perform testing procedures to evaluate muscle strength and range of motion. Then he or she must develop an exercise program to develop strength, coordination, balance, and activities of daily living (ADL) skills. If you worked in a school, you would also share with the doctor the responsibility of fitting and maintaining the children in braces, artificial limbs, or other special equipment.

Since the effectiveness of the program depends on parental cooperation, a great deal of this work involves parent instruction, demonstration, and conferences to interpret the child's changing needs and the therapies used to meet them.

Therapists working in children's programs must possess ingenuity and initiative as well as the knowledge of basic physical therapy principles and procedures. They must correlate the technique with the use of equipment and must often adapt the furniture such as chairs, desks, and wheelchairs to fit the needs of specific children. Mechanical aptitude is a great asset here.

Like the teachers in a school, therapists must share in other activities of the school. They attend staff meetings and conferences to interpret the capability and disability of the child in the classroom. Therapists share the philosophy of rehabilitation with the entire school faculty and assist them in the management of the child. Therapists also share in the responsibility for such nonphysical therapy duties as fire drills, bus duty, educational trips, and safety programs. Therapists usually serve on the committee to help screen children for admission to the special school and again to recommend transfer of children to regular schools.

In the school programs, the physical therapist is employed by the board of education or the board of health, by a private agency, or by the city as a civil servant. Whatever agency pays the salary, the therapist is entitled to all the benefits and privileges that teachers enjoy—annual salary increments, sick leave, retirement benefits, and summer vacations. Many find that having summers and holidays free offsets the generally lower pay of physical therapists working in the schools. This is especially good for therapists who are raising children of their own. In a typical school, the therapist works between 8:30 A.M. and 3:30 P.M., Monday through Friday, from

September until June. During these nine months, the therapist shares with the academic faculty of the school the job of watching children grow. Like the teachers of handicapped children, the physical therapist needs a great love for children as well as enthusiasm and patience. Because the therapists are away from professional colleagues while working in a school environment, they must possess added self-discipline to continue their own professional education.

Industrial Clinics

Industrial clinics are those associated with business or industry. Some large companies, for example, have small but well-equipped physical therapy departments to return injured employees to their jobs in the best possible condition and in the shortest possible time following an injury. Twenty-five percent of the injuries that happen on the job are hand injuries, but many are multiple injuries involving fractures, sprains, strains, dislocations, crush injuries, lacerations, amputations, ruptured muscles and nerves, and weakness resulting from injuries.

There are a variety of special considerations to keep in mind when considering work in an industrial clinic. First of all, the turnover of patients in these industrial clinics is rapid because no chronic conditions are treated and much of the work is preventive. The caseload is heavy and the tempo is fast, so the therapist must be adept at organizing large volumes of work. Second, the therapist working in industrial clinics must enjoy working largely with men and must be diplomatic, yet able to prod the patient to harder work. Finally, because there are many lawsuits filed by employees following industrial accidents, the industrial therapist must keep detailed and extensive records of progress and make frequent appearances in court.

Approximately ten years ago, the Volvo automobile factory in Sweden became alarmed by its number of industrial-related accidents, and it began a program to prevent, rather than to treat, injuries through better designs of industrial and business equipment. The program was so successful that other nations have copied it. This form of preventative design is termed *ergonomics*, and it has resulted in a great decrease in injuries and, consequently, cost.

Ergonomics is a relatively new and rapidly expanding area in industrial medicine and design. Therapists involved in this type of program will inspect equipment for placement, height, comfort, and other parameters, to minimize the workers' strain. The therapist will also conduct classes on body mechanics and seminars on the company premises.

Geriatrics

There are a number of different types of places a physical therapist or assistant might work with the geriatric patient population. Institutions or convalescent homes for the care of the aged are growing, both in size and number. Some older patients cannot return home because of the severity of a stroke or arthritis or the aftereffects of a fracture. Others cannot return simply because there is no one at home to care for them during the convalescent period after a fracture or operation. In addition, physical therapy departments in rehabilitation centers and curative workshops are similar to those in general hospitals treating a majority of orthopedic and neurological patients. In these centers, the patients live at home and commute by private or public transportation or by agency-operated buses. Finally, in some larger institutions a staff of qualified physical therapists is on hand to treat and to supervise treatments. In many institutions, however, the physical therapist serves as a consultant.

In geriatrics, the physical therapist delivers much the same kinds of treatment as in other areas. Older patients may receive heat, massage, exercise, walking training, and self-help activities to make them independent. The therapist may administer this treatment directly or teach assistants or other members of the hospital or nursing home staff to do this work with the patients.

The pace in a geriatrics center is slower because the patients move slower. They need more time for repetition of movement and more time to talk about their problems. In the geriatric setting, the therapist must stress the psychological aspects of care as much as the actual and physical care. He or she must emphasize the individuality of the patient and must strive constantly to reestablish the patient's self-confidence. The therapist must be on guard not to promise unrealistic goals to the weary older person.

Physical therapy with geriatric patients stresses strengthening and stretching exercises, balance, and coordination training. In this respect, it is similar to all the other aspects of physical therapy. It differs from hospital work, however, in the amount of contact that the therapist has with the patient's family and with representatives of other agencies in the field of health, education, and welfare. The therapist has less medical supervision, and, therefore, must plan more carefully for the patient's continued treatment program. He or she must also arrange for the patient's return to the doctor at the proper intervals.

Like the therapists in schools, those in rehabilitation centers must make adaptive equipment and must have teaching skill and the ability to motivate patients to greater challenges and success. The physical therapist assists the business office in ascertaining the cost of treatment and helps the social-service staff determine a patient's ability to pay for services. Because many older patients are on Medicare or Medicaid, discussing financial concerns and the patient's ability to afford assistive devices and medications may also be a part of the therapist's job.

In rehabilitation centers, the team approach to treatment is more important than any independent form of treatment. All the services unite to treat the patient as a whole, to restore function, and to aid in psychological adjustment. Many of the disabled who seek treatment in rehabilitation centers have conditions beyond the help of definitive medical care. These patients need a dynamic and coordinated program to teach them to live effectively within the limits of their disability, but to the maximum of their capabilities. The rehabilitation process continues until the patient attains the greatest possible degree of independence—not only physically but also socially, mentally, economically, and vocationally.

Private Practice

During the past few decades, there has been an increasing trend toward physical therapists developing private practices. In some states there had been a movement to force all therapists to be independent and to work in private practice, or in contractual agreements with large institutions and nursing homes, rather than as employees. The reason for this was an attempt to enhance the image of physical therapists as professionals.

One-third of physical therapists and one-fourth of assistants work in home health, outpatient rehabilitation centers, nursing homes, or clinics, or are self-employed. Some physical therapists are part of a consulting group. Most of those in private practice treat patients in a private office. These therapists pay all their own expenses: rent, electricity, gas, telephone, and so on. They buy all their own equipment and pay their employees, including assistants. They also make arrangements for vacation and sick-leave replacements.

The most frequent treatments physical therapists in private practice give are whirlpool, hot packs, ultrasound, diathermy, traction, massage, and therapeutic exercise. Most treatments average between thirty and forty-five minutes per patient, and most patients receive three treatments a week. The average private patient receives a total of eleven treatments, but 25 percent require more than fifteen treatments. The physical therapist in private practice works between eight and thirteen hours each day, but ten hours a day is the average. Therapists in private practice treat an average of twenty patients per day.

Although the physical therapist in private practice works longer hours, her or his income can be much higher than that of therapists working in hospitals or for agencies and institutions. This is the major reason for developing a private practice. Private practice also provides for greater freedom in structuring time. Obviously, the financial risk is greater, but so are the rewards of success. Although this type of physical therapy career is more financially rewarding, it lacks much of the excitement and personal and social contact of a hospital. It also lacks the opportunity for participation in medical staff meetings and for the training of students.

There are a variety of factors involved in being successful at operating a private physical therapy practice. A physical therapist needs at least three years' and preferably five years' experience before beginning a private practice. Therapists who leave facilities after a successful experience there and establish a practice in the same area have an easier time than those who organize a practice where they are unknown. The success of a therapist in private practice depends on many things: the size of the community, the number of doctors, the industrial enterprises, and the number of competing departments in the area. It also depends upon the attitude and the interest of local doctors in physical therapy. The ultimate success of a therapist depends, however, on the quality and quantity of his or her work, and on initiative, personality, and sales ability.

Some therapists who are self-employed in private practice have contractual arrangements with small hospitals and nursing homes. These small institutions, with between forty-five and two hundred beds, cannot afford the expense of a physical therapy department. Therefore they arrange for a private therapist to spend a certain number of hours or days each week in evaluating, testing, and developing treatment programs for the patients. The therapist must also teach the nurses, nursing assistants, aides, and orderlies how to perform certain follow-up care.

Consulting

Some physical therapists work as consultants to hospitals or clinics setting up physical therapy departments, to school districts, and to other institutions requiring the services of physical therapists.

The duties of the consultant are less those of patient care and more that of educator and business manager. The consultant must organize the physical therapy department, order equipment, arrange for clinical evaluations, develop treatment programs, outline them in writing, and teach the permanent staff. They make frequent reports to the referring doctors and to the administration about the department's growth and finances.

Consultants must have a minimum of two years of clinical practice, but most have had longer work experience in a variety of situations, including teaching and supervising.

In some areas, consultants work out of a central hospital, visiting the surrounding satellite hospitals. Other areas where consultants work today are public health departments, visiting nurse associations, regional health programs, heart programs, and many other agencies. Some consultants are self-employed and work under contract, but others are on salary. The fee arrangement will vary, depending on the locality and working hours.

Home Health Care

Physical therapy home health care is a viable and necessary option for a range of patients, both young and old. A patient who is chronically ill or permanently disabled sometimes can leave a general hospital and return home if he or she has follow-up physical therapy care in the home. Other patients may be able to stay out of hospitals if they can receive physical therapy in their homes. For some patients who cannot walk or who have other physical or emotional disabilities that make treatment in an ordinary department difficult or impossible, treatment in the home is necessary. A few patients lack transportation, and others must travel so far that the value of the treatment is counteracted by the difficult journey. A partial solution for these patients is treatment in the home.

The physical therapist has an obligation to serve as many people as possible, and one cannot ignore the many for the few. A home-care program is costly in time and productivity by comparison to treatment in a center. For this reason, a home-care program must be a teaching program, limited in time. It continues only long enough for the patient to adapt to the disability and for the family members to learn their role in positioning and exercising the patient and adapting the furniture and the house to the patient's needs.

The therapist must decide at the outset the best type of treatment for the patient. Does the patient require a dynamic rehabilitation program to improve his or her condition? Is the patient a candidate for maintenance or supportive care—for example, an exercise program that will keep the patient in the same place because the condition won't improve but should not become worse? Does the patient need only custodial care to prevent muscles and joints from getting stiff and the skin from breaking down into pressure sores? After the therapist has decided what type of care the patient needs, it is necessary to instruct the family in the exercise program. If the patient needs a dynamic program, the therapist may bring along portable equipment such as heat lamps, diathermy machines, ultrasound units, or weights to hasten the recovery period.

In a homebound program, the physical therapist helps the patient adapt to her or his disability and live with it. Therapists do more than merely give treatments; they must help the patient and family solve the problems of the patient. They must establish a rapport with the family, and they are frequently the family's only continuing contact with the doctor.

A therapist must have an automobile to treat homebound patients. Although it is possible to use public transportation, it is very impractical and time consuming. The number of patients a therapist treats will vary with the distance, driving time, and severity of the patients' problems.

Clinics for the Mentally Ill

The goal of physical therapy in a hospital for the mentally ill is to establish and keep the patient in continued contact with reality. The therapist provides patients with activities that may help them return to society as soon as possible in the best possible condition. Physical therapists working with the mentally ill use physical therapy treatments and apply specific psychological approaches to deal with this particular patient population.

Some patients with schizophrenia suffer from catatonia, a condition of marked muscular rigidity resulting in contractures at the joints. Usually patients with catatonia assume rigid, unchanging positions for extended periods of time. Physical therapists attempt to keep these patients' joints free and their muscles limber. Many of these patients also develop pressure sores from lack of movement. The therapist attempts to stimulate the patient into changing positions and frequently must treat pressure areas with various modalities. Other patients develop swollen legs, and the therapist will encourage these patients to move and to elevate their legs.

Specific treatments help patients overcome the problems that are confining them. Sometimes the patient lies in a sedative tub to relax. Other patients may be encouraged to play water polo to relieve their aggression or their abundance of energy. Another form of physical therapy treatment for the mentally ill patient is the salt glow, a vigorous massage in which salt is used instead of a lubricant to stimulate circulation.

The therapist working in a mental hospital must be gentle, kind, and able to understand the patient. He or she must be able to handle patients in a firm but just manner. A therapist working in this setting must be sincere because these patients can sense very quickly when a person is indifferent or insincere. Tact, diplomacy, and an understanding of the fears of these patients are prime requisites for this job.

Sports Medicine

Whether a professional team plays to earn money for the owners or a varsity team plays to enhance its school's image, all individuals on the team have a serious obligation to fulfill their assignments. The player, for example, must be in the best possible condition before the game and, if injured during the game, he or she must receive the best treatment available as quickly as possible to return to active competition. It's the physical therapist's job to treat and prevent the injury of those participating in a variety of sports.

Injuries are more common among high school and college athletes than among the professionals. This is because the amateur, who is primarily a student, does not have adequate time to devote to the necessary conditioning before competition and consequently is much more prone to injuries. In addition, although most accidents occur in football, soccer, and hockey—the more aggressive sports—injuries also occur in baseball and basketball.

Many physical therapists hold concurrent certificates as athletic trainers, and this enhances the job potential for them. Both amateur and professional teams have trainers who assist in the conditioning program but are also concerned with the care of the player following injury. In the past, trainers were former athletes who had acquired a smattering of knowledge about the treatment of trauma and orthopedic injuries. Today's trainer is a qualified physical therapist who has a good foundation in anatomy and kinesiology and, therefore, is better prepared to supervise the exercise program. More important, the physical therapist has knowledge of which treatment techniques are needed for fractures, lacerations, sprains, strains, dislocations, and torn cartilage in the knees. The physical therapist treats the injured player after referral by the team physician or another specialist, just as in a hospital, rehabilitation center, or in a private office.

The pace of life and work is fast. The job is an exciting one because the physical therapist travels with the team to all its engagements. The patients are young, strong, and healthy, so the outlook of the therapist is constantly optimistic. Besides being exciting and fun, the salaries in this specialty are relatively high.

Dance has grown in popularity in recent years, and today people of all ages are studying ballet and modern dance. Dancers can suffer from injuries just as serious as those experienced by players in competitive sports. In ballet, the dancer assumes positions that stretch muscles and joints far beyond normal limits. Injuries to the feet, ankles, and knees are common. Modern dance puts less strain on the feet and legs, but the leaps and falls can be hazardous. Some of the large dance companies have orthopedists and physical therapists on their staffs to treat dancers' injuries.

A new subcategory of sports medicine or sports therapy involves therapy for musicians. Many musicians suffer from sprains and strains in the upper extremities because of the intensive use of the arms while playing instruments. For these lovers of music, such treatment would have many benefits.

Foreign Assignments

If you are blessed or cursed with an incurable wanderlust, you can work as a physical therapist or assistant in a foreign land. In every nation of the world there are opportunities to live and work as a physical therapist or assistant. Your job can lead you to explore a different culture and learn its language, religion, philosophy, and social customs while you do important and necessary work.

If you want work experience in a certain nation, it is possible to obtain reciprocity (permission to work) if the other nation is a member of the World Confederation for Physical Therapy or WCPT (www.wcpt.org) and if the government of that nation permits foreigners to hold salaried positions. While the WCPT is a wonderful resource for researching global physical therapy initiatives, it does not offer information about working opportunities in other countries. For this type of information, you should go directly to physical therapy associations or organizations in the country of interest.

Foreign assignments are exciting, but they were not created for the opportunist who merely wants to use a work assignment abroad as a springboard to a free world tour. People who request help need the guidance of therapists who are dedicated to physical therapy, their patients, and their employers. The therapists who are chosen must be mature enough and unselfish enough to work long hours, side by side with the nationals, in the heat or the cold, teaching and helping them in a true spirit of humanity and good fellowship. American therapists serving abroad should attempt to live as much as possible as the people in the area live, and not demand special or unusually luxurious accommodations at the expense of their hosts.

The nature of your experience working abroad will vary from place to place. In Europe, where the ratio of physical therapists to the population is much greater than it is in the United States, the salaries of physical therapists are lower. It is also good to remember that the cost of living in most of the European nations is just as high or higher than the cost of living in America. The greatest need for physical therapists is in Africa, Asia, and South America. Therapists who work on any of these three continents find problems similar to those found at home and others that are very different. Language differences present the greatest problem. In Hindu and Muslim areas, male therapists may not treat female patients, and in some Muslim areas, even foreign women may not examine or treat a Muslim woman's legs. In all of the emerging nations, there is a great deal of leprosy, tuberculosis, polio, meningitis, and other diseases (which were rampant in the United States at the turn of the twentieth century). There is relatively little work done in cerebral palsy, in geriatrics, or in the treatment of chronic problems.

No matter where you go or under whose auspices you work, you will need a passport, visas, and an international health certificate, and it is good to have an international driver's license. You will need to be immunized against typhoid, typhus, tetanus, cholera, malaria, polio, and any other disease afflicting the nation where you will live. Before you leave the United States, you should take time to study the history, geography, religion, social customs, and, if possible, the language of the nation where you will work.

Most people who have worked in a foreign assignment have at one time, at least, gnashed their teeth in frustration over their inability to effect more rapid change. No matter who sponsored you, you are an unofficial diplomat of the United States. You must therefore hide your irritation and remember that the reason you are there is to help relieve suffering and promote good health, regardless of national or cultural differences.

The International Committee of the Red Cross (www.icrc.org) has sent physical therapists into several areas, but perhaps one of the most exciting assignments in its history was that of sending European, Australian, and American therapists to Morocco in 1960, when thousands of people became paralyzed after consuming contaminated cooking oil. The therapists screened the patients, tested them, and taught Moroccan assistants how to exercise them. You should check out the Red Cross's website for information on employment opportunities.

Teaching

Over the past thirty years, the field of physical therapy education has seen many changes. At one time, the earlier schools were attached to hospitals, and the instructors were usually part of the hospital physical therapy staff, who taught techniques after the doctors had laid the foundation in anatomy, physiology, and medical lectures. Today's university program has brought a sharp differentiation between the role of the teacher in the academic institution and the role of the practicing clinician. All faculty members in today's programs must have at least a master's degree, and a doctorate is necessary for school directors. The emphasis today is on the why of physical therapy, rather than on the how of four or five decades ago.

College and university educations have a variety of obligations. Teachers planning curricula must provide each student with opportunities to obtain a broad knowledge of anatomy, physiology, pathology, kinesiology, neurology, orthopedics, and medical principles, as well as proficiency in physical therapy techniques. University faculty must undertake research in addition to teaching. Teachers must be constantly concerned with changes in the profession and must anticipate the needs of the future and adjust the curriculum to meet the demands.

Physical therapy programs generally have two types of faculty members. One is the academic, full-time faculty member who teaches classroom subjects and is paid a salary by the university according to his or her position. The other is a clinical faculty member. These physical therapists work with students in the practical application of their knowledge. At various periods during the academic course and at the completion of it, the academic faculty arranges for the students to spend time in approved clinical settings, where well-qualified physical therapists observe, teach, and critique the students.

Research and Writing

The rate of growth in any profession depends upon the amount of information that research contributes to the profession. Physical therapy began as a service to patients, not as a body of knowledge.

Research came later and helped the practice of physical therapy become a profession.

Today, both in the academic halls and in busy clinics, therapists consider the how, the where, the why, and the when of the treatments that they have given for so many years. This systematic investigation of physical therapy is long overdue. Physical therapists must clarify what needs to be known and thus better prepare students for more extensive research in both science and in practice.

The physical therapist in research must cooperate with all the members of the rehabilitation team, but therapists must no longer rely upon other related bodies of learning to supply their knowledge. Specific research problems of physical therapy as distinct from other areas such as nursing, psychology, and orthopedics, are now receiving professional, focused research attention. Those who wish to learn how to research must enroll in proper courses in the large universities and join forces with the established investigators so they may learn to employ the necessary skills.

Writing and publishing the results of research is important because it informs others of the results. Physical therapists must reevaluate old material in the light of new knowledge and experience, read widely, and study the current literature carefully. They must report even minor tips in the practice of physical therapy that might help their fellow workers. They should report illustrative cases. In short, in both research and writing, a physical therapist must give old ideas a new examination and work steadily toward the growth of the body of physical therapy research literature needed today.

6

GETTING STARTED

THERE ARE A variety of factors that you must consider before you embark upon your new career as a physical therapist or a physical therapist assistant. One of the first decisions you must make after graduating from a physical therapy program is which is more important to you—a job in a particular hospital or living in a certain locality. Must you live in Boston, New York, or San Francisco? Do you want to make your home in a ski center in Colorado or a sailing area such as New England? Do you yearn for the perpetual summer of Arizona and Florida? Do you want to be by your family and friends or do you want to strike off on your own? No matter what part of the country you decide to live in, there's sure to be an appealing job somewhere in the near vicinity.

Job Hunting

After you decide where you want to live, you will then begin looking for the job that's best for you. Many new graduates accept positions in hospitals where they received a part of their clinical experience. These institutions are teaching hospitals and offer the new graduate excellent learning opportunities. The department director and the clinical faculty know the students and can observe which students are best fitted for the job requirements. Clinical students know which hospital has the type of cases that interest them most and the department structure that will help them perfect their knowledge. Students who want to obtain a job in such a hospital usually apply for their positions during their periods of clinical experience. They may be invited to join the staff of the clinical facility during their affiliation or very shortly after they leave it.

Job hunting is an adventure and, while it is usually quite nerve wracking, it can also be fun. One thing to keep in mind is that everyone who has a job once hunted for it, even the most intimidating directors of physical therapy departments. Unless you accept a position in one of the hospitals where you received your clinical experience, you should begin job hunting shortly before graduation so that you have a job lined up once you've passed your licensure examinations. Start by writing to the directors of the departments where you would like to work. Include a polished résumé along with your cover letter stating your expected date of graduation and licensure. There are a variety of books available that will help you craft and polish a résumé; it is a very good idea to buy at least one and put it to good use.

If you have always had a great yearning to work in a certain hospital or certain town, but find no opening listed, don't despair. Write to the hospital or to the organizations in the area. Few facilities are completely staffed, and the turnover is rapid enough in most departments that a job might very well open up for you. Remember, too, that many institutions with openings run advertisements only periodically and then wait for applicants. Some smaller hospitals that need staff just sit back and wait for a miracle—like you—because advertising isn't always effective.

Besides viewing websites and calling human resources departments of the hospitals, clinics, or rehabilitation centers you wish to work for, there are a variety of ways to find jobs. Some institutions delegate either a physical therapist or a personnel officer to interview students on college campuses during job fairs. Additionally, all physical therapy schools or departments have lists of positions available. These are compiled from letters sent to them by hospitals and institutions that need therapists. The APTA offers job listings and career information on its website (www.apta.org), as will other professional organizations. Job and career-based websites like careerbuilder.com and monster.com also offer job and résumé posting services, as well as a variety of information about careers. Finally, job listings can be found in trade journals such as those listed in Appendix C.

In addition to being a national organization, the American Physical Therapy Association has state-specific chapters that you should contact for additional information about jobs. Large or heavily populated states are further divided into districts. If the state chapter is divided into districts, each district has a placement committee and chairperson. These chairs keep up-to-date listings of all positions available in the area. They supply the list to any member of the American Physical Therapy Association. This service is free to both the recruiting institution and the physical therapist.

Choosing the Right Job

It is very important that you select a job that is well suited to you. Often the young therapist who performs poorly is unhappy because the work situation is not suited to her or his ability or personality.

Some people have a flair for working with children but lack the patience to handle geriatric patients; others are just the opposite. Some can perform outstanding work in a well-staffed center where the workload is light and therapists have unlimited time to devote to a few patients. The people in understaffed and busy clinics may become frustrated, morose, and often inefficient.

Often the tone of the department and the culture of the overarching organization make the difference in the successful performance of physical therapists. Some prefer to work where there is close and direct supervision by a physician or by the director and where the rules are clearly defined and strictly enforced. Others would rather work where they have free rein to use their imaginations, to improvise, and to make decisions within the framework of the rules of the profession.

It is important for all of us to heed the advice of Polonius in Hamlet. Polonius tells his son Hamlet, "To thine own self be true." This is as important in life as it is on a stage; as important today as it was in the sixteenth century. Recognize your abilities and your limitations, your likes and dislikes, and take the time to carefully analyze them to identify the kind of job that will most appeal to you. Don't play the martyr and work in a job just because someone is needed, knowing that you don't like working with a certain age group or a certain type of disability—or that you can't stand the boss. If you accept a job you really don't want, you will be personally unhappy, you will hate your job, you will reject your profession, and you will most likely not succeed in your field. If you choose a job you want, it will challenge you to make great contributions to your profession and to your community. Moreover, you will find yourself a bigger and better person because of it.

When you decide to accept an offer of employment, notify the director of the department as soon as possible. Then, either phone or write all the other institutions where you applied to inform them that you have accepted another position. You want to project a professional image, and as a professional you have responsibilities to others, including truthfulness and consideration. Physical therapy directors of the institutions you turn down or those you have applied to will appreciate your thoughtfulness and may remember you positively in the future. If the job you accept doesn't work out, you won't regret this small act of consideration.

Legal and Professional Requirements

In 1920, the American Physiotherapy Association established educational and professional qualifications for physical therapists. In the 1930s, the American Registry of Physiotherapists established its standards. During the years between 1920 and 1950, most hospitals and institutions required their physical therapists to be members of either or both organizations, because this membership meant that the therapists had completed an acceptable course in physical therapy and had passed a very difficult examination to qualify for registration.

The American Registry of Physical Therapists (ARPT) was disbanded in 1970. For approximately forty years it had functioned as an examining board to qualify physical therapists and, during that time, members encountered no problems in seeking employment in many different states. When state licensure became mandatory, the ARPT no longer fulfilled its purpose and was abolished. The American Congress of Physical Medicine, which had supervised the ARPT during its existence, continued to publish a monthly journal called the *Archives of Physical Medicine*. A descendent of this journal is alive and well today. The *Archives of Physical Medicine and Rehabilitation* is the official journal of the

American Congress of Rehabilitation Medicine and the American Academy of Physical Medicine and Rehabilitation.

Licensure

Some time ago, it became increasingly apparent that licensing would be necessary to establish standards of performance, because incompetence in this field is a threat to public safety. Each state enacted its own licensing laws, complete with standards of practice and regulations for practicing. Proof of graduation from a physical therapy program accredited by the Commission on Accreditation in Physical Therapy Education (CAPTE) and the successful completion of the examination provided by the state are the usual criteria for licensure.

Today the Federation of State Boards of Physical Therapy (www.fsbpt.org) administers the National Physical Therapy Examination (NPTE) for physical therapists and the National Physical Therapy Assistant Examination (NPTAE) for physical therapist assistants. All fifty states and three additional jurisdictions use the NPTE as one factor in the licensure or certification of physical therapists and physical therapist assistants. Some states also require physical therapists to pass a jurisprudence examination prior to licensure. This examination covers current state physical therapy statutes, rules, and regulations. You should review your state's official website and search the term "licensure" for additional details.

The NPTAE test is a well-constructed, up-to-date examination that contains content developed by professionally active physical therapists with the guidance of professional examiners. The content is meant to test the fundamentals that an entry-level physical therapist or physical therapist assistant should know upon graduation from an accredited program. You are allowed four and a half hours for the physical therapist examination and three and a half hours for the physical therapist assistant examination. There are 225 questions on the physical therapist examination and 175 items on the physical therapist assistant examination.

Obtaining and maintaining your license once you have passed the licensing examinations vary from state to state. State licensing fees are variable. In some they are nominal, but in others the cost is relatively expensive because of legal fees involving state licensure and amendments. Most states require physical therapists to show proof of completed continuing education to maintain and renew their license to practice, but the number of hours necessary to meet the requirements varies.

Not all states require licensure or registration for the physical therapist assistant to practice. The states that require licensure stipulate specific educational and examination criteria. Complete information on legislation and regulations governing physical therapy can be obtained from the state licensing boards. Additional requirements may include certification in cardiopulmonary resuscitation (CPR) and other first aid and a minimum number of hours of clinical experience.

Malpractice Insurance

Every health care worker, no matter which field he or she works in, must purchase malpractice insurance, which is also known as professional liability insurance. Many hospitals pay the cost of malpractice insurance for physical therapists in their inclusive insurance policies. However, physical therapists in private practice and in some agencies must purchase their own insurance protection. Because students also work with patients they, too, purchase malpractice insurance, even though they are typically covered under their clinical instructor's insurance. The rates vary with the type of work that a therapist or student engages in. Generally, malpractice insurance policies provide coverage for actual or alleged errors, omissions, negligence, breach of duty, misleading statements, and similar claims resulting from the performance—or nonperformance—of professional services. Malpractice suits against physical therapists, as with other health care professionals, are increasing, so obtaining this insurance is a must.

Advancement

Many physical therapy schools suggest that new graduates accept positions in large teaching hospitals in metropolitan areas. This is because a position offering a variety of experiences will help you decide in which area of physical therapy you want to specialize, if you are not yet sure. Teaching hospitals have a reputation for being more open to those who are less experienced. Workers at teaching hospitals tend to place lifelong learning and teaching in priority positions. In addition, metropolitan areas offer the benefit of greater numbers of employment options than do smaller communities.

Today an ambitious, eager, and dedicated therapist, even though comparatively young and inexperienced, may rise very quickly to a position of responsibility and prestige. An old Welsh proverb says, "The cream always rises to the top." Thus, the exceptionally well-qualified person will be singled out for promotions, for better positions, and for offices in professional organizations. The indifferent, lackadaisical, or negative personality will remain in a rut, plodding through life with neither challenge nor reward.

Of course, not everyone wants to be a chief in a large department. Many therapists want only to devote themselves to the service of humanity or to do research in one of the specialties. This need is great and the service they give is important. Remember, even in physical therapy we need more line workers than chiefs, so never look down on therapists who are not department directors.

American Physical Therapy Association

The American Physical Therapy Association (APTA) is a national association of physical therapists that was formed to standardize the developing education and service of physical therapists. This organization continues to define the function of physical therapists and to promote standards of service by developing educational requirements. It aids in planning the development of new facilities and the organization, administration, and curricula of new physical therapy schools. The American Physical Therapy Association promotes and protects the economic and general welfare of its members through governmental lobbying. It also offers continuing education credits and career development opportunities.

The APTA is divided into chapters, usually comprising states. Each chapter has a president and an executive board of the officers. Some large states have more than one chapter, while other large states prefer to divide into districts. Districts, like chapters, have officers, committees, and committee chairs. The smaller chapters and districts hold monthly meetings, which usually combine a business meeting with an educational program. Most chapters and districts sponsor evening and weekend workshops at cost for the members. Each year the chapters hold a two- to three-day conference combining business sessions, lectures, and recreational programs.

Membership fees vary depending on whether you are a student or a professional, a physical therapist or a physical therapist assistant, but they are quite expensive. You can expect to pay between $275 and $450 as a physical therapist and less for the other positions mentioned. While the fees may be substantial, many find membership in a professional organization beneficial, both in terms of tangible benefits and the prestige of being listed as a member.

The APTA publishes a monthly journal, *Physical Therapy*, that contains articles written by members, scientists, and physicians. The APTA also publishes the *PT Bulletin Online*. Links to these journals can be found in Appendix C.

Personal Qualifications

Everyone in a profession is eager to advance as rapidly as possible. Promotions and advancement bring salary increases, prestige, and greater opportunity. While it's important to possess self-confidence and strive to excel, you must also be realistic about the rate at which you will progress in your job. Every day you will add new tools and techniques to your arsenal of treatment, making you a wiser and more experienced physical therapist or therapist assistant. Experience is necessary for gaining knowledge and advancing in your field.

Success in physical therapy depends a great deal on how well suited you are to the field. Although there is no "typical" physical therapy personality type, personal qualifications make the difference between an outstanding therapist and an ordinary one, even though the two might have had identical educational training. Scientist and educator Dr. James Conant said, "Ideals, like stars, can never be reached, but we use them to chart our course." Several authors have written about the necessary qualities of a physical therapist, and Katherine Worthingham et al., in an article entitled "The Selection and Education of the Physical Therapy Student," give us excellent suggestions for the qualifications for a physical therapist.

In addition to the personal characteristics we mentioned in Chapter 2, there are several important qualities that nearly every good physical therapist possesses. Every physical therapist must have the ability to become a good teacher who can help the patient help himself or herself. The physical therapist must be capable of communicating with the patient and the family and must be able to draw information from the patient, hear what he or she has to say, and listen to the patient with silent understanding. Good physical therapists take responsibility for helping build their profession as well as their own personal futures. They will not submit to routine or uninspired performance of duties but will participate in research activities, as well as assuming responsibility for their share of the rehabilitation work.

Physical therapists must like people regardless of size, weight, color, creed, income level, or disposition. They must have friendly, kind, and patient personalities. They must be sympathetic, but not possess maudlin sympathy that destroys the working relationship. They must be dignified but not stuffy. They must have the emotional stability to be professional persons who perform their obligations during working hours without letting their personal lives interfere with their work. By the same token, they must not become so involved with their patients that they carry their patients' problems into their own personal lives. Their personalities must be both mature and flexible, so that they can vary the programs they administer; they must not let themselves become automatons.

Good working habits are especially important in careers that require both knowledge of scientific subjects and the ability to deal effectively with people. Physical therapists must be industrious, conscientious, neat, clean, punctual, attentive to details, and able to concentrate completely on their work. They must be able to organize a schedule because most departments carry heavy workloads. It is important that they keep accurate records and be meticulously honest with themselves and with others.

Physical therapists must possess leadership to influence those who look to them for guidance and support. They must also feel pride in accomplishment. To perform at the highest levels, they must keep abreast of new procedures and treatments. They should be able to assume the responsibilities and duties of all citizens, cultivating their minds as they study and serve the society in which they live.

Financial and Emotional Rewards

In the past, salaries of all workers in the health field were lower than salaries in business and industry for positions requiring a comparable amount of formal education and demanding much more responsibility in the form of being responsible for the health of a human life. During those years, personnel directors had a favorite cliché: "This is the price you pay for the privilege of serving humanity." Fortunately, those years of low salaries never deterred or influenced anyone who wanted to become a physical therapist. Admittedly, the long hours of hard work, the great responsibility, and the low salaries did have a discouraging effect on many therapists whose college classmates were earning four times as much in business careers.

Since that time, we have seen dramatic changes in the salary scale and in the personal benefits for physical therapists. Today salaries compare favorably with, and often exceed, those for other positions demanding similar educational backgrounds and responsibility. According to the *Occupational Outlook Handbook*, in 2002 the median annual earnings of physical therapists were $57,330. The middle 50 percent earned between $48,480 and $70,050. The lowest 10 percent earned less than $40,200, and the highest 10 percent earned more than $86,260. Median annual earnings in the industries employing the largest numbers of physical therapists in 2002 were as follows:

Home health care services	$62,480
Offices of other health practitioners	$58,510
Offices of physicians	$57,640
Nursing care facilities	$57,570
General medical and surgical hospitals	$57,200

According to the Bureau of Labor Statistics, median annual earnings of physical therapist assistants were $36,080 in 2002. The middle 50 percent earned between $30,260 and $42,780. The lowest 10 percent earned less than $23,530, and the highest 10 percent earned more than $48,910. Median annual earnings of physical therapist assistants in 2002 were $35,870 in general medical and surgical hospitals and $35,750 in offices of other health practitioners.

Salaries alone, low or high, could never compensate a physical therapist for the physical expenditure of energy and the emotion spent on patients year in and year out. A mountain climber braves the hazards of a precipitous ascent in thin air because "the mountain is there." Mary McMillan, founder of the APTA, once said, "There was a job to be done, and I was there." The physical therapist invests his or her life in the patients because they, too, "are there." Patients are like magnets, drawing those who must devote their lives to the rehabilitation of the disabled.

Physical therapy is more than a way of earning a living; it is a way of life. There is a story about the famous English architect, Sir Christopher Wren, that can be applied to physical therapy. Sir Christopher was inspecting the building of a cathedral that he had designed. He stopped to talk with the workers, and he asked three of them what they were doing. The first person answered, "Cutting a piece of stone." The second replied, "Earning five shillings a day." The third said, "Helping to build a cathedral." Like the third man, a physical therapist does not exercise a hip joint, or earn $60,000 a year, but helps people to rebuild lives. There is no way to measure the amount of emotional rewards this will provide you.

Working Conditions

Physical therapists practice in hospitals, clinics, and private offices that have specially equipped facilities, or they treat patients in hospital rooms, homes, or schools. In the United States, hospitals, institutions, and organizations that provide care for the sick and disabled usually provide pleasant working conditions. Most American hospitals have central heating during the winter and provide air-conditioning in the summer. Some hospitals provide parking, meals, and laundry, either at cost or free, for their staffs.

Departments vary in size depending upon whether the department was designated as physical therapy before a new building was erected or whether it was stuck in the only space available in an aging and obsolete structure. Space may be generous or limited; departments may be crowded or spacious. In many institutions, physical therapy departments are located on a portion of a single floor. Sometimes, a department occupies several floors of an entire wing or, possibly, a whole building. Some departments have a number of spacious treatment and dressing rooms, exercise areas, and private offices. In other departments, there are cubicles sectioned off by curtains in one or two large rooms. Some departments must use corridors for gait training and waiting rooms, while others have luxurious furnishings. Most departments are light, airy, clean, and bustling.

Therapists who treat patients in the patients' homes may find circumstances there varying from fully staffed mansions to squalid conditions in a high-poverty area, depending upon whether the service for homebound patients is a private practice or a public health service. The therapist engaged in a homebound service may spend a great deal of time traveling through summer heat or winter blizzards. At other times, however, the traveling therapist may pass through the fragrant apple blossoms of the spring and the breathtaking foliage of fall. The point is, climate and weather must be taken into consideration.

Therapists who volunteer for foreign service will not always find working conditions pleasant and comfortable, but relatively few therapists work overseas.

There is no such thing as a typical work schedule for a physical therapist because there is so much flexibility in the field. In general, however, the majority of employed therapists work forty hours a week. Traditionally, this has been Monday through Friday from 8:30 A.M. to 5:00 P.M. Some general hospitals are open on Saturday mornings, with rotation of a minimum staff. These persons are then given a half-day off during the week or are paid time and a half for the overtime. Increasingly, departments are open on weekends. In some California institutions the departments are open twenty-four hours a day, seven days a week. Some physical therapists work evening and weekend hours to accommodate patients. The usual labor laws regarding luncheon and morning and afternoon breaks, legal holiday time, and vacation scheduling apply to physical therapists, although self-employed therapists do not have to observe the labor laws.

Advantages and Disadvantages

In a job, career, or profession, will you ever find a utopia? In any field there will be moments that are dull, routine, tedious, and irritating. No job can promise you a forty-hour workweek filled with constant mental stimulation, emotional reward, and recognition of your knowledge and ability. Every career has something special to offer you, and, simultaneously, every career lacks something you desire. You must exchange one thing for another. Only you can determine what you want to gain and what you prefer to reject.

Disadvantages exist in physical therapy just as in any other field. Specifically, the work is physically, mentally, and emotionally tiring. You will be lifting patients who cannot move, and this is hard physical labor. The workload will be heavy, not only because patients today are getting heavier, but also because many departments are inadequately staffed. Sadly, the shorter-staffed the department, the more urgent the need for additional recruits, but the more difficult it is to find replacements.

Despite the importance that physical therapists place on body mechanics, a sudden motion by a patient may catch a therapist off guard and cause an injury. Occasionally a therapist has been hospitalized in traction, braced, or operated on as a result of an injury suffered in the line of duty while performing routine tasks. There is usually some form of worker's compensation that will be given the physical therapist by the hospital or institution while he or she is healing.

A day's work can leave you zapped of energy because you are superimposing your will upon your patients' in an effort to draw from them the response you want. Often it is an action that they don't want to undertake, so you must achieve your result by positive encouragement, never by scolding and criticism. This emotional aspect is definitely more fatiguing than the physical handling of patients.

The advantages of physical therapy as a career far outweigh the disadvantages. First, the job potential is constantly increasing. During the past few years, salaries have doubled and even tripled in some areas. Professions always offer prestige to those who practice them. Other health workers respect physical therapists for their role on the rehabilitation team. The lay public surrounds physical therapists with an aura of glamour because they help people walk again.

Conclusion

While we covered a lot of ground in this book, we did not discuss the fundamentals of constructing a résumé and cover letter or tips for conducting a good job interview. This level of detail is simply beyond the scope of this book. That said, there are a variety of useful and informative books on the shelves and online that will help you do just these things. Your career resource center staff or your local or school librarians are excellent sources of information for books on interviewing, cover letters, and résumés. If you want to dog-ear your own copy, do a search on www.amazon.com and read the reviews of books in this subject to help you narrow your choices. Once you have several books, be sure to read them thoroughly and put them into practice. There will be many other applicants vying for your ideal job, so you should do what you can to make yourself stand out.

I hope this book has opened up to you and demystified the world of physical therapy. It is a field with incredible growth opportunities, both personally and financially, and it is one full of challenges and rewards. As Mary McMillan said, "Physical therapy isn't always easy. It's the hard knocks that bring out the best timber in us. Who wants a soft job, anyway?"

APPENDIX A

Accredited Physical Therapy Programs

Alabama

Alabama State University
www.alasu.edu

University of Alabama at Birmingham
www.uab.edu/dopt

University of South Alabama
www.southalabama.edu/alliedhealth/pt

Arizona

Arizona School of Health Sciences
www.ashs.edu

Northern Arizona University
www.nau.edu/hp/dept/pt

Arkansas

Arkansas State University
http://pt.astate.edu

University of Central Arkansas
www.uca.edu/divisions/academic/pt

California

California State University–Fresno
www.csufresno.edu/physicaltherapy

California State University–Long Beach
www.csulb.edu/colleges/chhs/physical-therapy

California State University–Northridge
http://hhd.csun.edu/pt

California State University–Sacramento
www.hhs.csus.edu/pt

Chapman University
www.chapman.edu/wilkinson/pt

Loma Linda University
www.llu.edu/llu/sahp/pt

Mount St. Mary's College
www.msmc.la.edu/pt

Samuel Merritt College
www.samuelmerritt.edu

University of California–San Francisco
http://itsa.ucsf.edu/~ptprog

University of the Pacific
www.uop.edu

University of Southern California
www.usc.edu/pt

Western University of Health Sciences
www.westernu.edu/xp/edu/cahp/dpt_about.xml

Colorado

Regis University
www.regis.edu/dpt

University of Colorado Health Sciences Center
www.uchsc.edu/pt

Connecticut

Quinnipiac University
www.quinnipiac.edu/x1025.xml

University of Connecticut
www.alliedhealth.uconn.edu

University of Hartford
www.hartford.edu

Delaware

University of Delaware
www.udel.edu/pt

District of Columbia

Howard University
www.howard.edu

George Washington University
www.gwumc.edu/healthsci/programs/pt/pt.htm

Florida

Florida Agricultural and Mechanical University
www.famu.edu

Florida International University
http://physicaltherapy.fiu.edu

Nova Southeastern University
www.nova.edu/pt

University of Central Florida
www.cohpa.ucf.edu/health.pro/ptms.cfm

University of Florida
www.phhp.ufl.edu

University of Miami
www.miami.edu/pt

University of North Florida
www.unf.edu/coh/cohatpth.htm

University of St. Augustine for Health Sciences
www.usa.edu

Georgia

Armstrong Atlantic State University
www.pt.armstrong.edu

Emory University
www.rehabmed.emory.edu/pt

Georgia State University
www.gsu.edu

Medical College of Georgia
www.mcg.edu/sah/pt/index.html

North Georgia College and State University
www.ngcsu.edu

Idaho

Idaho State University
www.isu.edu/departments/dpot

Illinois

Bradley University
www.bradley.edu/academics/ehs

Governors State University
www.govst.edu/mpt

Midwestern University
www.midwestern.edu/il-pt

Northern Illinois University
www.ahp.niu.edu

Northwestern University
www.nupt.northwestern.edu

The University of Illinois at Chicago
www.ash.uic.edu/pt

Indiana

Indiana University
www.dpt.indiana.edu

University of Evansville
http://pt.evansville.edu

University of Indianapolis
http://pt.uindy.edu/dpt

Iowa

Clarke College
www.clarke.edu

Des Moines University
www.dmu.edu/pt

St. Ambrose University
www.sau.edu/pt

The University of Iowa
www.medicine.uiowa.edu/physicaltherapy

Kansas

University of Kansas Medical Center
www.kumc.edu/sah/pted

Wichita State University
http://chp.wichita.edu/pt

Kentucky

Bellarmine University
http://lansing.bellarmine.edu/pt/index.asp

University of Kentucky
www.uky.edu

Louisiana

Louisiana State University Health Sciences Center
http://alliedhealth.lsuhsc.edu/physicaltherapy

Maine

Husson College
www.husson.edu/pt

University of New England
www.une.edu/shp/pt/index.html

Maryland

University of Maryland–Baltimore
http://pt.umaryland.edu

University of Maryland–Eastern Shore
www.umes.edu/pt

Massachusetts

American International College
www.aic.edu/web/ptherapy/index.htm

Boston University
http://web.bu.edu/sargent

MGH Institute of Health Professions
www.mghihp.edu

Northeastern University
www.northeastern.edu

Simmons College
www.simmons.edu/shs

Springfield College
www.spfldcol.edu/pt

University of Massachusetts–Lowell
www.uml.edu/dept/pt

Michigan

Andrews University
www.andrews.edu/phth

Central Michigan University
www.chp.cmich.edu/pt

Grand Valley State University
www.gvsu.edu/pt

Oakland University
www.oakland.edu/shs/pt

University of Michigan–Flint
www.umflint.edu/pt

Wayne State University
www.wayne.edu

Minnesota

College of St. Catherine
http://minerva.stkate.edu//offices/academic/dpt.nsf

College of St. Scholastica
http://grad.css.edu/pth

Mayo School of Health Related Sciences
www.mayo.edu/mshs/pt-ptmp-rch.html

University of Minnesota
www.physther.umn.edu

Mississippi

University of Mississippi Medical Center
http://shrp.umc.edu/programs/pt.html

Missouri

Maryville University of St. Louis
www.maryville.edu/academics/hp/pt

Rockhurst University
www.rockhurst.edu/pt

Southwest Baptist University
www.sbuniv.edu/pt

St. Louis University
www.slu.edu/colleges/ah/pt

University of Missouri, Columbia
www.umshp.org/pt

Washington University
http://pt.wustl.edu

Montana

University of Montana–Missoula
www.umt.edu/pt

Nebraska

Creighton University
http://pt.creighton.edu

University of Nebraska Medical Center
www.unmc.edu/physicaltherapy

New Jersey

Richard Stockton College of New Jersey
http://loki.stockton.edu/~mpt

Rutgers, The State University of New Jersey
www.umdnj.edu/shrpweb/programs/mpt

University of Medicine and Dentistry of New Jersey/
   Kean University/Seton Hall University
http://shrp.umdnj.edu/physicaltherapy

New Mexico

University of New Mexico
http://hsc.unm.edu/som/physther

New York

The College of Staten Island
www.csi.cuny.edu

Columbia University
www.columbiaphysicaltherapy.org

Daemen College
www.daemen.edu/academics/physical_therapy/default.html

D'Youville College
www.dyc.edu

Hunter College
www.hunter.cuny.edu/schoolhp/pt

Ithaca College
www.ithaca.edu/pt

Long Island University–Brooklyn Campus
www.brooklyn.liu.edu/dpt

Mercy College
http://grad.mercy.edu/physicaltherapy/index.htm

New York Medical College
www.nymc.edu/sph/pt

New York University
www.nyu.edu/education/pt

The Sage Colleges
www.sage.edu

State University of New York Downstate Medical Center
www.downstate.edu

State University of New York Upstate Medical University
www.upstate.edu/chp/pt

Stony Brook University
www.hsc.stonybrook.edu/sohtm_ptindex.cfm

Touro College
www.touro.edu/shs/pt/pt.asp

Utica College
www.utica.edu

North Carolina

Duke University
http://dpt.dukehealth.org

East Carolina University
www.ecu.edu/pt

The University of North Carolina at Chapel Hill
www.med.unc.edu/mahp/physical

Western Carolina University
www.wcu.edu/aps/pt

Winston–Salem State University
www.wssu.edu

North Dakota

University of Mary
www.umary.edu

University of North Dakota
www.medicine.nodak.edu/pt

Ohio

Andrews University–Dayton
www.andrews.edu/phth

Cleveland State University
www.csuohio.edu

Medical College of Ohio
www.mco.edu/depts/pt/index.html

The Ohio State University
www.amp.ohio-state.edu/pt

Ohio University
www.ohiou.edu/phystherapy

University of Cincinnati
www.cahs.uc.edu/departments/physicalt.cfm

The University of Findlay
www.findlay.edu/academics/cohp/phth/index.html

Youngstown State University
http://bchhs.ysu.edu/dpt/dpt.html

Oklahoma

University of Oklahoma Health Sciences Center
www.ah.ouhsc.edu/rehab

Oregon

Pacific University
www.pt.pacificu.edu

Pennsylvania

Arcadia University
www.arcadia.edu/pt

College Misericordia
www.misericordia.edu

Drexel University
www.drexel.edu/cnhp/depts/rehab/programs/dpt

Duquesne University
www.healthsciences.duq.edu/phyth

Gannon University
www.gannon.edu

Neumann College
www.neumann.edu

Saint Francis University
www.francis.edu/academic/undergraduate/physther/pthome.shtml

Slippery Rock University of Pennsylvania
www.sru.edu/depts/pt

Temple University
www.temple.edu/pt

Thomas Jefferson University
www.tju.edu

University of Pittsburgh
www.shrs.pitt.edu/physicaltherapy

University of the Sciences in Philadelphia
www.usip.edu

University of Scranton
http://academic.uofs.edu/department/pt/default.html

Widener University
www.widener.edu/ipte

Rhode Island

University of Rhode Island
www.ptp.uri.edu

South Carolina

Medical University of South Carolina
www.musc.edu/pt

University of South Carolina
www.sph.sc.edu/dpt

South Dakota

University of South Dakota
http://med.usd.edu/pt

Tennessee

Belmont University
www.belmont.edu/pt

East Tennessee State University
www.etsu.edu/cpah/physther/index.htm

University of Tennessee at Chattanooga
www.utc.edu/physicaltherapy

University of Tennessee Health Science Center
www.utmem.edu/physther

Texas

Angelo State University
www.angelo.edu/dept/physical_therapy

Hardin-Simmons University
www.hsutx.edu/academics/phys_therapy

Texas State University–San Marcos
www.health.txstate.edu/pt

Texas Tech University Health Sciences Center
www.ttuhsc.edu/sah/program_pages/mpt_home.htm

Texas Woman's University
www.twu.edu/pt

University of Texas at El Paso
www.chs.utep.edu/pt/home.html

University of Texas Health Science Center at San Antonio
www.uthscsa.edu/sah/pt

The University of Texas Medical Branch at Galveston
www.sahs.utmb.edu/programs/pt

University of Texas Southwestern Medical Center at Dallas
www.utsouthwestern.edu/physicaltherapy

U.S. Army–Baylor University
www.cs.amedd.army.mil/baylorpt

Utah

University of Utah
www.health.utah.edu/pt

Vermont

University of Vermont
www.uvm.edu/physicaltherapy

Virginia

Hampton University
www.hamptonu.edu/academics/schools/science/pt/index.htm

Marymount University
www.marymount.edu/academic/healthprof/pt

Old Dominion University
www.odu.edu/dpt

Shenandoah University
www.su.edu/pt

Virginia Commonwealth University
www.vcu.edu/pt

Washington

Eastern Washington University
www.ewu.edu/pt

University of Puget Sound
www.ups.edu/pt

University of Washington
http://depts.washington.edu/rehab/education

West Virginia

West Virginia University
www.hsc.wvu.edu/som/pt

Wheeling Jesuit University
www.wju.edu/academics/departments/pt.asp

Wisconsin

Carroll College
http://depts.cc.edu/ah/pt

Concordia University Wisconsin
www.cuw.edu/dpt

Marquette University
www.marquette.edu/chs/pt/index.html

University of Wisconsin–LaCrosse
http://perth.uwlax.edu/pt

University of Wisconsin–Madison
www.orthorehab.wisc.edu/pt

Appendix B

Accredited Physical Therapy Assistant Programs

Alabama

Bishop State Community College
www.bscc.cc.al.us

George C. Wallace Community College
www.wallace.edu

Jefferson State Community College
www.jeffstateonline.com

South University
www.southuniversity.edu

Wallace State Community College–Hanceville
www.wallacestatehanceville.edu

Arizona

Gate Way Community College
www.gwc.maricopa.edu/curriculum/pta

Arkansas

Arkansas State University
http://pt.astate.edu

Northwest Arkansas Community College
www.nwacc.edu/academics/alliedhealth

California

Cerritos College
www.cerritos.edu

De Anza College
www.bhs.deanza.edu/pta

Loma Linda University
www.llu.edu/llu/sahp/pt

Ohlone College
www.ohlone.edu/instr/phys_ther

Sacramento City College
www.scc.losrios.edu/~sah/physther

San Diego Mesa College
http://intergate.sdmesa.sdccd.cc.ca.us/physical_therapy/index

Sonoma College
www.sonomacollege.com

Colorado

Arapahoe Community College
www.arapahoe.edu/deptprgrms/pta/index.html

Morgan Community College
www.morgancc.edu

Pueblo Community College
www.pueblocc.edu

Connecticut

Naugatuck Valley Community College
www.nvcc.commnet.edu/allied_health/allied_healthframe.shtml

Delaware

Delaware Technical and Community College
www.dtcc.edu/owens

Delaware Technical and Community College
www.wilmington.dtcc.edu/wilmington

Florida

Broward Community College
www.broward.edu

Central Florida Community College
www.cfcc.cc.fl.us

Daytona Beach Community College
www.dbcc.cc.fl.us

Florida Community College at Jacksonville
www.fccj.edu/prospective/programs/data03_04/222A.html

Gulf Coast Community College
www.gc.cc.fl.us

Indian River Community College
www.ircc.edu/atircc/progrcs/health/phyther/phyther.html

Keiser College
www.keisercollege.cc.fl.us

Lake City Community College
www.lakecitycc.edu

Manatee Community College
www.mccfl.edu

Miami Dade College
www.mdc.edu

Pensacola Junior College
www.pjc.edu

Polk Community College
www.polk.edu/instruct/mash/alliedhealth/pta/index.htm

Seminole Community College
www.scc-fl.edu

South University
www.southuniversity.edu

St. Petersburg College
www.spcollege.edu/hec/pta

Georgia

Athens Technical College
www.athenstech.org/academicaffairs/alliedhealthnursing/pta

Darton College
www.darton.edu/programs/alliedhealth/pta.htm

Gwinnett Technical College
www.gwinnetttechnicalcollege.com

South University
www.southuniversity.edu

Hawaii

Kapi'olani Community College
http://programs.kcc.hawaii.edu

Idaho

Idaho State University, College of Technology
www.isu.edu/departments/pta

Illinois

Black Hawk College
www.bhc.edu

College of DuPage
www.cod.edu

Illinois Central College
www.icc.edu

Kaskaskia College
www.kaskaskia.edu

Lake Land College
www.lakeland.cc.il.us/models/physicaltherapistasst087.htm

Morton College
www.morton.edu

Oakton Community College
www.oakton.edu/acad/career/pta_p1.htm

Southern Illinois University
www.siu.edu

Southwestern Illinois College
www.swic.edu

Indiana

Brown Mackie College
www.brownmackie.edu

Ivy Tech State College
www.ivytech.edu/muncie/health.htm

Ivy Tech State College–Northwest
http://gar.ivy.tec.in.us

University of Evansville
http://pt.evansville.edu

University of Indianapolis
http://pt.uindy.edu/dpt

University of Saint Francis
www.francis.edu/newsfc/academic/undergrad/health/physther

Vincennes University
www.vinu.edu

Iowa

Indian Hills Community College
www.ihcc.cc.ia.us

Kirkwood Community College
www.kirkwood.edu/healthscience/pta/pta.html

North Iowa Area Community College
www.niacc.edu

Western Iowa Tech Community College
www.witcc.com

Kansas

Colby Community College
www.colbycc.edu/?m=4&s=69&1=123

Kansas City Kansas Community College
www.kckcc.cc.ks.us

Washburn University of Topeka
www.washburn.edu/sas/ah/pt-assist/index.html

Kentucky

Hazard Community College and Southeast Community College
www.hazcc.kctcs.edu

Jefferson Community College
www.jcc.kctcs.edu

Madisonville Community College
www.madcc.kctcs.edu/~pta

Somerset Community College
www.somcc.kctcs.net

West Kentucky Community and Technical College
www.allied.westkentucky.kctcs.edu/pta

Louisiana

Bossier Parish Community College
www.bpcc.edu

Delgado Community College
www.dcc.edu

Our Lady of the Lake College
www.ololcollege.edu

Maine

Kennebec Valley Community College
www.kvcc.me.edu

Maryland

Allegany College of Maryland
www.ac.cc.md.us/department/phyther.htm

Baltimore City Community College
www.bccc.edu

Carroll Community College
http://faculty.carrollcc.edu/pta

Montgomery College
www.montgomerycollege.edu

Massachusetts

Bay State College
www.baystate.edu/pta

Becker College
www.beckercollege.edu

Berkshire Community College
www.berkshirecc.edu/flash.html

Massachusetts Bay Community College
www.massbay.edu

Mount Wachusett Community College
www.mwcc.mass.edu/html/default.html

North Shore Community College
www.northshore.edu

Springfield Technical Community College
www.stcc.edu/ieindex.asp

Michigan

Baker College of Flint
www.baker.edu

Baker College of Muskegon
www.baker.edu/visit/muskegon.html

Delta College
www.delta.edu/health/pta/index.html

Finlandia University
www.finlandia.edu

Henry Ford Community College
www.hfcc.edu/programs/sheets/physicaltherapistassistant.asp

Kellogg Community College
www.kellogg.edu/pta

Macomb Community College
www.macomb.edu

Mott Community College
www.mcc.edu/slbc_pta.shtm

Minnesota

Anoka Ramsey Community College
www.ank.tec.mn.us

College of St. Catherine
http://minerva.stkate.edu//offices/academic/dpt.nsf

Lake Superior College
www.lsc.mnscu.edu/academics/programs/pta

Mississippi

Hinds Community College
www.hindscc.edu

Itawamba Community College
www.icc.cc.ms.us

Meridian Community College
www.mcc.cc.ms.us/newhome

Pearl River Community College
www.prcc.edu/cattecp.htm

Missouri

Linn State Technical College
www.linnstate.edu

Missouri Western State College
www.mwsc.edu

Ozarks Technical Community College
www.otc.edu/degrees/alldhlth/pta/index.htm

Penn Valley Community College
www.kcmetro.cc.mo.us/specialprog/physther.html

St. Louis Community College at Meramec
www.stlcc.edu/mc

Nebraska

Clarkson College
www.clarksoncollege.edu

Northeast Community College
http://alpha.necc.cc.ne.us

Nevada

Community College of Southern Nevada
www.ccsn.edu

New Hampshire

Hesser College
www.hesser.edu

New Hampshire Community Technical College
www.nhctc.edu

New Jersey

Bergen Community College
www.bergen.edu/ptap

Essex County College
www.essex.edu

Mercer County Community College
www.mccc.edu

Union County College
www.ucc.edu

New Mexico

San Juan College
www.sanjuancollege.edu

New York

Broome Community College
www.sunybroome.edu

Genesee Community College
www.genesee.edu/healthcareers/pta

Herkimer County Community College
www.hccc.suny.edu/academics/divisions.htm

Kingsborough Community College
www.kbcc.cuny.edu

LaGuardia Community College
www.lagcc.cuny.edu/ptaprogram

Mercy College
http://grad.mercy.edu/physicaltherapy/index.htm

Nassau Community College
www.ncc.edu/dptpages/ahs/pt/ptframe1.html

Niagara County Community College
www.niagaracc.suny.edu/lsd/pta.html

Onondaga Community College
www.sunyocc.edu

Orange County Community College
http://orange.cc.ny.us/pta

State University of New York College of Technology at Canton
www.canton.edu/can_start.taf?page=study-program-pta

Suffolk County Community College
www.sunysuffolk.edu

Touro College
www.touro.edu/shs/pt/pt.asp

Villa Maria College of Buffalo
www.villa.edu

North Carolina

Caldwell Community College and Technical Institute
www.caldwell.cc.nc.us

Central Piedmont Community College
www.cpcc.edu/health-sciences/physical-therapist-assistant

Fayetteville Technical Community College
www.faytech.edu

Guilford Technical Community College
http://technet.gtcc.cc.nc.us/academic/health/pta.htm

Martin Community College
www.martin.cc.nc.us

Nash Community College
www.nashcc.edu

Southwestern Community College
www.southwest.cc.nc.us

North Dakota

Williston State College
www.wsc.nodak.edu

Ohio

Clark State Community College
www.clarkstate.edu

Cuyahoga Community College
www.tri-c.edu/pta

Hocking College
www.hocking.edu

James A. Rhodes State College
www.rhodesstate.edu

Kent State University–Ashtabula
www.ashtabula.kent.edu/ptat/ptat.htm

Kent State University–East Liverpool
www.kenteliv.kent.edu

Lorain County Community College
www.lorainccc.edu

Marion Technical College
www.mtc.edu

North Central State College
www.ncstatecollege.edu/academics/healthsci/pta/physther.html

Owens Community College
www.owens.edu/academic_dept/health_tech/pta/index.html

Professional Skills Institute
www.proskills.com

Shawnee State University
www.shawnee.edu/academics/hsc/pta/index.html

Sinclair Community College
www.sinclair.edu/academics/alh/departments/pta/index.cfm

Stark State College of Technology
www.starkstate.edu/academics/health/ptassttech.htm

University of Cincinnati
www.cahs.uc.edu/departments/physicalt.cfm

Zane State College
www.matc.tec.oh.us/programs/pta.htm

Oklahoma

Carl Albert State College
www.carlalbert.edu

Murray State College
www.mscok.edu

Northeastern Oklahoma A&M College
www.neoam.cc.ok.us

Oklahoma City Community College
www.okccc.edu/health/pta.html

Southwestern Oklahoma State University
www.caddokiowa.com/academics/pta.htm

Tulsa Community College
www.tulsacc.edu/page.asp?durki=166

Oregon

Mount Hood Community College
www.mhcc.edu

Pennsylvania

California University of Pennsylvania
www.cup.edu

Central Pennsylvania College
www.centralpenn.edu

Community College of Allegheny County–Boyce Campus
www.ccac.edu

Harcum College
www.harcum.edu

Lehigh Carbon Community College
www.lccc.edu

Mercyhurst College
http://northeast.mercyhurst.edu/programs_of_study/associate_
degrees.htm#pt

Mount Aloysius College
www.mtaloy.edu

Pennsylvania State University–DuBois
www.ds.psu.edu

Pennsylvania State University–Hazleton Campus
www.hn.psu.edu

The Pennsylvania State University–Mont Alto
www.ma.psu.edu/~pt/index.htm

The Pennsylvania State University–Shenango
www.shenango.psu.edu

University of Pittsburgh at Titusville
www.upt.pitt.edu/upt_pta

Rhode Island

Community College of Rhode Island
www.ccri.edu

South Carolina

Greenville Technical College
www.greenvilletech.com

Midlands Technical College
www.midlandstech.edu/phystherapy

Trident Technical College
www.tridenttech.edu/rehab/pta.htm

South Dakota

Lake Area Technical Institute
www.lakeareatech.edu

Tennessee

Chattanooga State Technical Community College
www.chattanoogastate.edu/allied_health/ahmain.asp

Jackson State Community College
www.jscc.edu/allied

Roane State Community College
www.roanestate.edu/keyword.asp?keyword=pta

South College
www.southcollegetn.edu

Southwest Tennessee Community College
www.stcc.cc.tn.us

Volunteer State Community College
www.vscc.cc.tn.us

Walters State Community College
www.ws.edu

Texas

Amarillo College
www.actx.edu/~phys_therapy/-12k

Austin Community College
www.2.austin.cc.edu

Blinn College
www.blinn.edu/twe/pta/index.htm

Del Mar College
www.delmar.edu

El Paso Community College
www.epcc.edu

Houston Community College System
www.hccs.edu

Kilgore College
www.kilgore.edu

Laredo Community College
http://laredo.edu

McLennan Community College
www.mclennan.edu/departments/hsp/pta

North Harris Montgomery Community College
www.mc.nhmccd.edu

Odessa College
www.odessa.edu/dept/pta

San Jacinto College South
www.sjcd.edu

South Texas College
www.stcc.cc.tx.us/nah

St. Philip's College
www.accd.edu

Tarrant County College
www.tccd.edu/pta

Wharton County Junior College
www.wcjc.edu

Utah

Provo College
www.provocollege.edu

Salt Lake Community College
www.slcc.edu/pages/1027.asp

Virginia

Jefferson College of Health Sciences
www.jchs.edu

Northern Virginia Community College
www.nvcc.edu/medicalpta

Tidewater Community College
www.tcc.edu/academic/divisions/healthprofessions/pta/index.htm

Wytheville Community College
www.wc.cc.va.us

Washington

Green River Community College
www.greenriver.edu/programinformation/physicaltherapist
assistant.htm

Spokane Falls Community College
www.sfcc.spokane.cc.wa.us

Whatcom Community College
www.whatcom.ctc.edu/instr/pta.htm

West Virginia

Fairmont State Community and Technical College
www.fairmontstate.edu

Marshall University
www.marshall.edu/ctc

Wisconsin

Blackhawk Technical College
www.blackhawk.edu

Gateway Technical College
www.gatewaycc.edu/curriculum/pta

Milwaukee Area Technical College
www.milwaukee.tec.wi.us

Northeast Wisconsin Technical College
www.nwtc.edu

Western Wisconsin Technical College
www.wwtc.edu/wwtcstudents/healthmenu.asp

Resources for Additional Information

YOU WILL FIND the following organizations, journals, and websites helpful as you research a career in physical therapy. Contact those that interest you.

Organizations

American Congress of Rehabilitation Medicine
www.acrm.org

American Physical Therapy Association
www.apta.org

Bureau of Labor Statistics
www.bls.gov/home.htm

Federation of State Boards of Physical Therapy
www.fsbpt.org

International Committee of the Red Cross
www.icrc.org

National Association of Disability Evaluating Professionals
www.nadep.com

U.S. Department of Education
www.ed.gov

World Confederation for Physical Therapy
www.wcpt.org

Journals

Archives of Physical Medicine and Rehabilitation
www.archives-pmr.org

Journal of Orthopaedic and Sports Physical Therapy
www.jospt.org

Pediatric Physical Therapy
www.pedpt.com

Physical Therapy: Journal of the American Physical Therapy Association
www.ptjournal.org

PT Bulletin Online
www.apta.org/bulletin

Websites

www.careerbuilder.com
www.finaid.org
www.monster.com
www.pediatricphysicaltherapy.com
www.physical-therapist.com
www.physicaltherapist.com
www.scholarships.com

About the Author

BERNICE KRUMHANSL WAS a physical therapist with approximately five decades of professional experience. She received her Bachelor of Arts degree from Notre Dame College of Ohio, in Cleveland, and a certificate in physical therapy from the Cleveland Clinic Foundation. Her continuing education included short courses in arthritis, cystic fibrosis, orthopedics, neurology, proprioceptive neuromuscular facilitation, lower extremity prostheses, manipulation, cardiac care, burns, personnel management, acutherapy, yoga, the use of computers in physical therapy, education, muscle energy, and craniosacral therapy.

Ms. Krumhansl was also in private practice in Cleveland, Ohio, where she served as assistant professor of physical therapy at the Ohio College of Podiatric Medicine. She obtained earlier clinical experience as a staff physical therapist in the cerebral palsy unit of the Association for the Crippled and Disabled, and as the chief physical therapist at St. Alexis Hospital in Cleveland. For thirty-four years, she was Director of Physical Therapy at St. Luke's Hospital in Cleveland, where her responsibilities included both clinical and administrative duties, as well as the supervision of the students from several baccalaureate and associate degree programs.

In addition to this book, Ms. Krumhansl published approximately seventy articles on physical therapy, history, travel, and writing techniques; four radio scripts; and three juvenile short stories. She also presented more than two hundred slide lectures on her medical and personal experiences in Asia to benefit Christian medical missions in India.

A freelance writer with expertise in careers in both the liberal arts and sciences revised this edition.